ICE UNDER
SNOW

Published by Piscataqua Press
32 Daniel St., Portsmouth, NH 03801
www.piscataquapress.com

ISBN: 9781729496725

Printed in the United States of America
Cover photo by: depositphotos/blasbike

ICE UNDER SNOW

A memoir of identifying and confronting abuse and pedophilia

Josephine May

For Clara, Andrew, and Jason,

I love you.

Love, Mom

"*Some people write to make a living; others to share their insights or raise questions that will haunt their readers; others yet to understand their very souls. None of these will last. That distinction belongs to those who write only because if they did not write they would burst... These writers give expression to the divine — no matter what they write about.*"

Anthony de Mello

Could I Have this Dance for the Rest of My Life?

"Hi Josephine! How are you doing? I'm calling to ask if you will be a bridesmaid in my wedding."

"Yes!"

Me. *A bridesmaid!* I am so excited!

It's 1986 and my feathered hair is a neatly trimmed bob. I'm feeling insecure about my smile, knowing the gap between my big front teeth has only recently begun to close.

Everything about the wedding day is bright and cheerful! Canopy-covered tables fill the parking lot at the end of a private driveway in front of an old New England mansion. Friends and family bustle around, arranging vases of fresh flowers. Familiar fragrances fill the air as caterers serve lobster, lamb, water, wine, and champagne. Bright sunshine illuminates the carefully prepared scene, highlighting the beaming bride and groom where they sit at the head table, surrounded by the wedding party.

The bride and groom step into the center of the dance floor overlooking the ocean, for their first dance. Anne Murray's voice rises, as it has over all past and will over all future weddings of Evelynn's siblings: "Could I have this dance for the rest of my life?"

Family and celebration were normal features of my upbringing. I happily anticipated filling my life and my

i

children's lives with many positive traditions. Life's challenges provided me with a path I never expected. Things didn't go wrong until later...

1

Normal

An experience of collective pain does not deliver us
from grief or sadness; it is a ministry of presence.
These moments remind us that we are not alone
in our darkness and that our broken heart is
connected to every heart that has known
pain since the beginning of time.

Brené Brown
Braving the Wilderness

On April 21, 2011 my husband went to jail for molesting our daughter. It was shocking to me when this man, who I had learned to accept wasn't very emotive or agreeable, was more than just a difficult personality, he was a sexual predator. This realization was doled out in parts, each successively more shocking than the previous, until his behaviors became his own downfall.

Growing up as the daughter of two attorneys, both devout Catholics, naturally my childhood ambition was to become an attorney and have the kind of relationship I observed my parents sharing. My mother enrolled in pre-law when she was 41. I was only in sixth grade then, but still the strongest kid on the football field—and the fastest on the track. My mother showed me who I could become: tough, smart, educated, faithful, and undaunted by any challenge.

I was raised in Massachusetts, the youngest child in my family, and one in an extended family of 30 grandchildren. Part of the philosophy behind a large family is that you will follow the path of those who have come before you. With lots of older cousins and three older siblings, I had many successful family members to emulate. I watched and learned from them all. And there was never a dull moment.

Faith played a large part in my childhood. It seemed normal to me. It was all I knew. Both sets of my grandparents were Catholic. They prayed the rosary and hung pictures of the saints on their walls. We went to church every Sunday. In the early 1980's, as a kindergartener, I would walk over to church by myself if my parents had gone to an earlier mass and I didn't have a sibling available to take me. To be part of a religious community felt natural. Priests were family for us, and the church was a safe place of worship and friendships.

It wasn't until I was grown up that I realized other families didn't have nearly as many weddings, anniversaries, cookouts, Christmas parties, Easter parties, birthday parties, and weekend gatherings as our family. And that everyone didn't enjoy constant company and someone to help you with any problem you had. I didn't realize how lucky I was to be able to visit with two grandmothers who lived in the same town as me. It was a way of being that I assumed I would carry on into adulthood. I couldn't imagine any other kind of life.

Spending time with my dad was so special to me. I was proud to be his sidekick, happily donning my overalls and work boots when it was time to go to Jim's garage, or when I'd be called on to stack wood for the fireplace, fix a leaky bathroom faucet, or build a table. My parents had diverse interests, and I was happy to be with them, whatever they might have been doing.

In school, I hung out with the same friends from kindergarten through eighth grade, many of whom still hold a place in my heart. As people do, we all grew up and went our own ways, eating our slices of humble pie or tasting success, or both.

About the time my mother was finishing her law degree, I was finishing high school. My golden years of summers on the coast—collecting horseshoe crabs, fishing with my family on the boat, jumping in the dunes and exploring the castle at Crane's Beach with my siblings, playing tag with family friends—were just ending. A new life of sneaking cigarettes with high school friends waited for me on a near horizon.

During the late 1980s, my father was heavily invested in the real estate market. When the Red Sox lost the 1986 World Series, you could walk out on your back porch and see grown men crying. When the real estate market crashed a few years later, the feeling in our home was like the Sox defeat, only worse. We lost our beach and lake property and had to leverage the house we were living in to pay for my father's business offices.

My parents struggled to get by, the tension and sadness and fear they carried were palpable. Only later would I take full measure of their fears: the threat of being unable to keep a roof over our heads or put food in the fridge, of no longer being able to pay for college for four kids and my mom. I'm also not sure that I understood the social implications or possible embarrassment they must have felt as they scrambled to get by after their life's work imploded, leaving a crater to somehow climb out of. It took them a long time to recover.

This experience was a glimpse of how I would later in life come to see money—as not only a force for fear and uncertainty, but, in the wrong hands, a tool for coercion and extreme exploitation. My parents managed to find a way through, though, and, by the time I left home, had successfully pulled the family out of debt.

While still in high school, I was hired to be a lifeguard at a historic New England pond. During my first week on the job, my innocence and youthful sense of invincibility would become forever altered. It was a sunny day and the pond was filled with swimmers. As we were doing our four o'clock shift change, a loud whistle drew my attention to the water's edge. The lead lifeguard was carrying to shore the lifeless body of a six-year-old boy. I would only later come to realize the way in which the shock and grief of this trauma influenced my choices as I was entering young adulthood. A sudden awareness that life was tenuous and short overcame me.

Breaking my parents' rule against chasing after boys, I called a guy I had a crush on—the boy who would one day become my husband and the father of my children.

Cal was a year behind me in school, a skinny kid with glasses and wild hair, younger than me and totally non-threatening. His affection was comforting. Cal had an eccentric, earthy way about him, but he was smart, too, the recipient of several academic awards. His sense of humor was dry and simple. If you blinked, you might miss one of his witty remarks.

Cal hung out with a different crowd from the friends I had spent most of my middle and high school years with. His family was different from my own, too—eccentric and permissive. They drank wine with every dinner and always invited a full table of young people to join them. It felt good to be an immigrant in this foreign domain. I was intrigued by this new way of being and began to rebel against my upbringing.

The first weeks of Cal's and my relationship were fun and carefree. We spent time with other kids from our high school, attended graduation parties and pool parties, and took little wilderness excursions around the edges of our hometown. Cal seemed not to be in any way intimidated or controlled by authority. He dreamed big and had the smarts to make things happen for himself.

Cal's fearlessness was impressive. He was willing to try anything. We started dating just after he'd returned from an extended trip overseas with one of his best friends, an adventure he'd made happen by planning ahead and saving up.

My guy was adventurous, intelligent, and confident. I worried about nothing when I was around him. When I looked for my reflection in his cool surface, I found a smart and special girl looking back at me.

Our differences seemed to draw me closer to who I wanted to be, a stable person without a lot of chaos in my life. While my parents would ultimately be successful at rebuilding their lives, the last six years with them had shaken my foundation, and I sought out relief in stability.

Cal brought me certainty and peace. He calmly and methodically thought through every decision. He planned and prepared for life. This was a luxury and a much-needed tutorial for me. After a few months of dating him, I was convinced there could be no better person for me in the entire world. I loved everything about him. His funny teeth, his big bird-nest hair, his scrawny body, his wit, his charm, his very presence made my heart glow.

We dated through the summer until I headed off for my freshman year at a small liberal arts college in Vermont. Cal stayed behind to finish his final year of high school.

Being away at school brought new freedom and possibilities beyond those I had known. I was relieved to be free of my parents' oversight, my mother's distracted do's and don'ts as she tried to manage our hectic lives, and my father's well-meaning advice. I left behind childhood and embraced freedom; taking with me running and Cal.

Competitive running was a part of my life in middle school, high school, and college. The experience of eating up the miles, the contrast between my body's chemistry when I set out and how I feel at the end of a run, is still something I enjoy.

Running

When I was 12-years-old, my middle school received an invitation to send a runner to compete at a cross-country race two counties over. Since I'd been winning all the local races, the gym teachers chose me to represent our school. My mom and dad were taken by surprise when a few days before the big race I mentioned I had been selected.

Other than the cross-country events that occurred in my town a couple of times a year, I didn't have much experience with competitive running at this point in my life. I'd never traveled so far to compete—in any sport—much less seen this particular course.

My parents drove me over to the race site, while I sat in the back seat, wondering to myself, "Will I finish strong?" I picked at the loose rubber sole of my dirty white Keds, wishing I had real running shoes. Finally, I closed my eyes and longed to be on the starting line, ready to begin and end this pain of not knowing how I would perform.

We pulled up to the middle school. "Hey there!" Mr. Shore, our track coach, was heading toward us from the other side of the parking lot wearing a white polo and blue slacks—school colors that matched my own shirt and shorts. Behind him trotted Coach Hayes, the high school varsity track coach. "Oh no," I thought. He sported a blue windbreaker with the school logo. He looked at my shoes and shook his head. Mr. Shore handed me my race number and four pins. He put his hand on my shoulder and turned me in the direction of a START banner across the way.

"C'mon," he said kindly. "They're just beginning the course orientation now."

The race official described the route, but my head was spinning, looking around at the other runners and I didn't see anyone I knew. And nobody else was wearing Keds. Suddenly, I really wanted to win this race. Runners moved up to the starting line. Even at age 12, I lined myself up in the front row. If one of these runners was slower than me, I didn't want that person getting in my way. Not everyone was running to win.

The gun went off and I headed out, consciously controlling my speed. By this early point in my running career, my mind had figured out how to win races. My body hadn't yet learned what to do with all of that adrenaline at the beginning of a race. I felt tired already—exhausted from the overwhelming pressure I had been placing on myself. I ran out, kept my pace. The air stung my lungs and cramped my stomach. I had to will my heavy legs to bend and unbend.

Finally, I hit my stride. My body settled down and my Keds began to meet the ground in an even rhythm. I could feel the roots, lumps of soil, rocks, and clumps of slippery leaves through the thin soles of my shoes. Leaves crunched under my feet. Triumph began to rise inside my chest as my legs moved on autopilot to maintain my lead.

Suddenly, everything felt wrong. Spectators lined the race path about 20 yards over to my right. But I was looking at their backs. I'd lost the course! My legs stopped. At that moment, one of the spectators happened to turn around and catch sight of me.

"You're off the course," he yelled. "Go back the way you came!"

"Th-thank you," I gasped and turned to backtrack.

Off to my left, two numbered runners, separated from one another by about six feet, approached. With a lead of roughly 10 steps, my feet rounded a corner onto a long downhill, straight stretch. In my peripheral vision, my eyes took in spectators lined up on both sides of the path leading to the finish. A cheer went up as I started down the hill. There was no one in front of me!

The man who had given me directions, gave me a wave just as my chest broke the tape. I collapsed into my dad's arms. Mr. Shore put a towel over my head and my mom handed me food and water. I heard another school's coach ask, "When is that girl getting to high school?"

Somehow, with the unexpected help of a stranger, I'd managed to win the race.

Derailed Plans

Successful people follow their instincts
beyond the emotions of their failures.

T.D. Jakes
Pastor and Author

The freedom of the Vermont mountains was a breathtaking experience for me as a college freshman in the fall of 1992. The self-driven life of my athletics and the friends I had chosen for myself were a fulfilling combination. Life was bringing me good things!

Academically, my focus was on becoming fluent in a foreign language and securing my sophomore year abroad. I maintained my relationship with Cal, but by the beginning of my second year away it had begun to feel different, enclosing.

Cal graduated from high school and was accepted at Princeton University.

One weekend, we were driving back to Vermont when he stopped at a ticket booth and collected our turnpike pass. When we arrived at the toll on the other end and he couldn't find our ticket, he blamed me.

The relationship had enough geographical distance that there wasn't a consistency in our interactions. I didn't have enough time to experience the pattern of emotional abuse that played out throughout the remainder of this relationship both in the marriage and after it ended. As an 18-year-old woman, I was not sophisticated enough to know that his blaming nature was not only something he would never grow out of, it would get worse. He never took responsibility for his behaviors or the crimes he was convicted of. He would later delight in the power that the court gave him to use "scorched earth" tactics as a means to avoid responsibility, and to blame and to batter through litigation.

In my naiveté I saw his blaming and criticizing as something that needed a sympathetic heart to love out of him. "If he could learn to trust my good intentions, he will love me even more for my loyalty."

Looking back, I wonder why particular moments made a permanent home for themselves in my memory. If these images could be so durable as to return repeatedly over the years, how was it possible I failed to grasp their significance at the time they were happening?

My sophomore year in college brought with it a series of successes on the cross-country team. Over the summer, I had trained and taken off weight, with a goal of winning every race in the upcoming season. I accomplished that goal, dropping a full minute off my 5K time. My coaches began to talk about sending me to Nationals for my division.

Alongside the happiness of winning repeatedly arose the subtle discontent that accompanies the end of a relationship. As spring approached, I began contemplating the best way to cut Cal loose. Then he drove up one day and surprised me with a visit. I felt a little bad because our relationship had been so close and I didn't want him to be hurt. Our daughter was conceived that weekend.

On April 1, 1994, Easter Sunday, the pregnancy test came back positive.

Driving along Interstate 89 one night, Cal suggested, "We don't have to do this right now." But I knew I didn't have a choice—*I had a child in me.* "Doing this" was a decision that I had already made. Who did he think he was talking to? Before we'd ever been intimate, we had discussed the possibility of pregnancy, and he knew I would have a baby if I ever did get pregnant. I could feel the little life inside me. I was the only protection this life had.

The discovery of how alone I was in the pregnancy was almost more than I could bear. Cal suddenly seemed not to know me at all, or care about my feelings. His cold-hearted view of life cut sharply across the fiber of my being. The thin black veil of ice on interstate 89 suddenly looked even darker. Never had the Vermont winter felt so cold.

As the months passed, an eerie nausea crept into my 20-year-old body, accompanied by vomiting 24 hours a day during my final exams. To this day, my stomach turns when I hear any mention of Jane Austen's *Mansfield Park*, the assigned reading that I listened to on cassette tape when I was too sick to hold a book.

Over spring break, I left Vermont to attend Evelynn's baby shower; she was having a baby too. When I discovered I was pregnant, I first told her, then my parents, then my siblings. I knew Evelynn would be supportive of me, and telling my parents before my siblings shielded me somewhat from my brother and sisters' reactions.

Evelynn understood what I was up against with this unexpected pregnancy. She offered me compassion and love. She was raised with the same foundational understanding that a woman who has sex outside of wedlock loses her value. I was young, unwed, and pregnant, and this was a scenario that our family was not going to look favorably upon.

I told my parents on Parents' Weekend, my sophomore year in college; I was about 4 weeks along. I can still remember telling my mom that I needed to talk to her and my dad after a dinner with all my college friends and their parents. My dad, looking like a middle-aged James Dean, was laying on the hotel bed with his white t-shirt and jeans on and my mom was wearing a turquoise and pink windbreaker with matching pants. I sat with them on the bed and held their hands and I explained that I was going to have a baby.

In a very gentle, kind voice my mother said, "You don't mind if we don't say anything for a minute?" My father muttered something under his breath while he curled his short hair around his finger, where he now has a bald spot. Dad said some things that I blocked out of my mind because I had an image of myself, of how I wanted him to view me. I was his youngest daughter and he spent a lot of time with me when I was a little girl, time that I cherished. I looked up to him. Now, he had to reconcile with every opinion that had ever been impressed upon him about a young woman who has sex and gets pregnant out of wedlock. He was worried that all my dreams were over.

Telling my siblings that I was pregnant went in the order of middle sister Adele, brother Harvey, older sister Alice. Alice was like a second mother, only stricter at times. Adele was like a friend. She was excited to meet the baby. Harvey didn't know what to think; he just felt badly for me. Alice was 26 years old and newly engaged, Adele was 23, in business school and living in the Fens, Harvey was 25 and just entering Suffolk Law School.

We were all just beginning our adult lives and the news of my unexpected pregnancy was shocking.

On a summer evening, early in my pregnancy, my siblings left me standing in the kitchen as they departed for a night out. They didn't invite, possibly because a pregnant girl couldn't drink alcohol or because they were embarrassed to be in my company. This was one of the first times that I felt real shame and exclusion. Alice was as upset as my father. Adele had her life planned out. She's a fixer and a doer and the pregnancy was something she didn't know how to approach. Harvey was caring and would spend time talking to me. He knew I was alone and afraid and that I was cut off from my school in Vermont and my friends. Making new friends would not be easy for me now.

I became very dependent on my own understanding of the world at 20, and on my child's father who was all of 19 years old. I felt very alone.

Cal and I lived in campus housing in Vermont that summer—an intense few months. I increasingly found myself on tenterhooks as he criticized me over meaningless incidents. He was argumentative about the meals I chose and invariably punitive about their cost. At a pizza parlor, I wanted to leave a good tip for the waitress on our $9 pizza. When I put down $2, he grabbed the money off the table, purposely berating my math skills.

The summer of 1994 was notoriously hot. The old TV in our shared dorm room flashed images of O.J. Simpson and his murdered wife and her lover. I instinctively dulled any connection my mind wanted to draw between my life and Nicole Brown Simpson's.

One of those summer evenings, Cal and I were discussing his plans for my future which did not resonate with my own plans. His ego needed constant assuaging and he became very angry and hostile, displaying his hair-trigger temper. This communication process was a key feature of how I lost touch with my own feelings because his emotions and behaviors were dangerous and threatening. During our argument he kicked the bed where I was resting. A young woman passing by knocked on the dorm-room door to see if I was ok. I answered in my nightgown, speaking words and using a tone I knew would restore our privacy. I was embarrassed by my circumstances and the way I was being treated.

"Is everything ok?"

"Oh yeah, everything is fine. Thank you for asking."

I shut the door and went back to my hell. He lay in his bunk, absorbed in his feelings. I began to make plans for the fall that didn't include him, but he fought against that.

"If you are not willing to come to Princeton, you'll need to give the baby up for adoption," he ordered. "If I can't be with the baby, then you shouldn't be either."

After we recounted this conversation to the student therapists we were counseling with on campus, they both agreed: "A baby needs its mother."

Cal was separating the baby out from my body before she was even born. He was claiming rights to the baby, saying what should be done with her. He was saying that if I wasn't moving my pregnant body to Princeton and raising the child with him on the campus and transitioning to school in New Jersey, then neither one of us should have the child.

I held out, hoping for a life raft to rescue me from this life I had been swept up in. I just wanted to survive the summer and move on. I told myself, *This is the tough part. It will get better.* Cal remained impervious to my physical suffering as well as the psychological anguish I was going through as I struggled to let go of the life I had planned for myself since I was a little girl.

I was a beautiful and strong young woman with a bright future, still figuring out what I wanted to do with my career. I loved languages and had enrolled in both French and advanced Spanish courses. Also, I tried out for a play hoping to get involved with theatre. The world was at my fingertips and I was just starting to get a taste of it. I had also envisioned a future with a husband who adored me, and I him. What I had was coercion.

Looking back, I now realize how he wielded shame and embarrassment to trap me in our relationship. I could not erase from my thoughts the desperation I'd witnessed on the faces of parents whose children I had babysat over the years—adults consumed by the needs of their infants and toddlers. It appeared difficult for them to have even minimal flexibility or mobility. They were stuck. Now I could only anticipate a similar future.

My well-connected family must have sensed how miserable I was with Cal in Vermont. Miraculously, I was offered a paid internship with a State Representative my sister had once worked for. I made the difficult choice to leave my wonderfully caring and supportive cross-country coaches, my cross-country ski team, and all that I had been excited to grow into and learn about and become in Vermont. But the internship felt like the life raft I had been waiting for, and I didn't hesitate to jump into it. I left my small liberal arts college and showed up at the Massachusetts legislature pregnant and awkward.

I was very aware of my belly protruding with new life as I sat in meetings amid other interns my age. I now had no idea who I was and how to present this unfamiliar version of myself to others.

I traded in my running shorts for a maternity dress. I had trouble, a lot of trouble, accepting my changing figure—the loss of my runner's body. I lived north of Boston and took the train to the city—an hour-long ride every morning. One day, a nice guy I knew from high school sat down next to me.

"What are you having?" he asked.

"I don't know," I said, "but I hope it's a girl."

He paused, looking down at my belly.

"You probably wouldn't want *her* to have to go through this."

For a second, before I realized he was talking about the pregnancy, I thought he had seen right through me to my troubled life.

"Yeah, really," I said, deciding, either way, his comment rang true.

As the commuter train rumbled down the tracks, I found myself coming to terms with the fact that my old life plan had become derailed. I had no blueprint for how to carry on as an unwed mother. But, even as I struggled with a painful loss of self, the light of the new life I was bringing into this world was something I was sure of. I loved my baby. In the midst of my suffering, I was learning an important lesson: that love can arise out of even the most difficult circumstances. I believed and still believe the words I whispered to my baby every day I carried her and that I often say to her to this day: "Clara, you are here to bring light to the world."

I wasn't alone in struggling to accept who I was becoming. My father, too, was having to let go of the daughter that he had so many dreams for. A man of his day, he did his best to come to terms with the pregnant young woman who was taking the place of his capable, athletic daughter.

A little over a year later, in 1996, I would make it to Nationals on Boston College's women's cross-country team. I was sharing a hotel room with a scholarship athlete when I broke down in tears of joy over my success. "I've reached my dream."

Education, Motherhood, and Cross-country Running

Our sport becomes not just what we do but an integral symbol — on all levels — of who we are.

Joan Benoit Samuelson
Gold Medalist, 1984 Summer Olympics

In the fall of 1994, during my third trimester, I enrolled at Boston College, taking night classes, with the intention of going full time to finish my Bachelor of Arts degree on time. I moved in with my parents, about an hour's commute to the BC campus. They had wanted me to go to Merrimack College. It was both of their alma mater, and my dad was teaching evening law classes there at the time. My mind was set on trying out for the Boston College women's cross-country team.

I had visited the BC campus and researched courses and discovered that I could participate on the NCAA Division I women's cross-country running team by enrolling in Boston College's evening school program. I was fortunate to have all my credits transfer.

I commuted to Boston for classes several evenings a week in my family's old 1975 Chevy Nova. It didn't have a radio, so I passed the time talking to my unborn baby, reflecting on my aunts and grandmothers who had journeyed on from this world.

Sometimes my mother, who was an attorney in Boston, would come to campus with me, sitting next to me in class as I finished up the first semester of school at Boston College and the third trimester of my pregnancy. In poetry class, the notebook resting on my stomach moved every time the baby tossed and turned.

Clara was born in mid-December, one week after I completed my finals.

My daughter came into this world healthy and strong, nursing right away. When she was escorted to the nursery so that I could rest, and I thought I heard her cry, I got up and immediately brought her back to sleep by my side.

In January, I enrolled full time for the spring semester. My daughter was five weeks old. I held Clara on my lap while interviewing childcare providers, adapting to my new role as Mommy. I continued to nurse her for 12 weeks, until I could wait no longer to get back into running condition. The hormones that naturally pour into your system when you're nursing make for softer ligaments and would increase my risk of injury.

I was hoping to pick up with collegiate indoor track that winter but, with a full course load and a newborn, I knew it would take me longer to be ready. Clara was eight months old when I walked on to the Boston College women's cross-country team. In the fall of 1995, our uniforms resembled bathing suit bottoms with tank tops. I was 120 lbs. on a 5' 6" frame and my body felt light and speedy as I ran toward a new kind of future with my child, invigorated and determined to be a good mom.

But, even with my many years of running experience, I couldn't help but feel intimidated. The team was halfway through the season before my home life became a topic. We were on the bus returning from a competition at the University of Maine when a guy on my team asked, "What do you do during the day when you're not in class?"

"I take care of my nine-month-old daughter," I replied.

He looked not just surprised but like he wanted to escape through the bus's emergency exit, and I couldn't ignore the hush that came over my other teammates as my words carried through the bus.

I was initially concerned I would be taken less seriously as a competitor if my peers became aware that I was a mother. But, by this point, I was regularly among the top 10 women athletes on the team. I soon began to bring Clara to races with me on good weather days. As it turned out, the coaches and my teammates delighted in watching her, with her big blond curls, toddling around the race perimeter in Franklin Park.

When I could get some free time, I would take her out with me in her running stroller. I cherished these hours of feeling strong and focused on something that was healthy for both of us. I had her first pair of running sneakers picked out in my mind. They were going to be pink, white, and grey. I planned on giving them to her on her 4th birthday. But it turned out that, at that age, my daughter was more interested in anthills and Barbie dolls; she hadn't gotten into running—yet! (Later, in her first year of high school, she would run the fastest quarter mile in Alaska.)

Clara spent time in day care three days a week. Cal would drive from New Jersey every weekend to take care of her while I competed in track and cross-country meets. She remained my greatest gift and first priority. At the same time, running proved to be the thing that kept me present and balanced as I found my way through the first year of parenting.

Clara and I lived with my parents while Cal was away at school. When he came home, we all stayed at his mother and stepfather's house. I studied and wrote while the baby slept at night. Some of this time was spent writing journals documenting Clara's life, from my pregnancy through her fifth year. These journals included all of Clara's milestones, funny things she said, as well as my concerns, hopes and dreams for her. I was so excited to share these journals with her when she got married and became a mother too.

I was proud of our young family and its newfound stability and began to believe my hopes for Cal to become a caring partner and father could come true.

I looked forward to getting up every morning to run. I had my team to train with and races to compete in. My pregnancy and relationship with Cal had taken a toll on my identity and now I thrived on being among the strongest competitors at the college level, pushing my body to its limits. I had my daughter and my schoolwork, too. It was a lot—not perfect in every way, but fulfilling. I had managed successfully to graft my new life as a parent onto my old identity and was beginning to grow a healthy new variation of myself.

We followed the typical training schedule, with two hard workouts a week and races on the weekends. I vacillated between placing number 9 and 10 on our team. Though my father loved Clara and helped with her care, his disappointment in me was still palpable at times. In 1996, as I was leaving for Nationals in Iowa with the team, I walked down the narrow staircase from the third floor of my family's century-old home in the early morning and encountered my father at the kitchen table. I sat down with him.

"I'm nervous," I confessed. I was competing against elite athletes, including several I had run with and against in high school who were going to college on scholarships.

"Why?" he asked. "This is what you wanted, isn't it?"

I was worried his once unshakeable pride in me might never return.

I began to think more about my choices, for the first time seeing in my personality a lack of willingness to promote myself—to get the best deal for myself. I wondered if this common variable of failing to value myself lay under both my earlier decision about where to go to college and my current choice to stay involved with Cal.

My parents supported my running career but were concerned about finances when it came to putting their fourth child through college. In my senior year of high school, University of Connecticut had expressed interest in me because I was a top athlete on my team. But with no real sense of direction I didn't pursue the opportunity. I now recognize the role my insecurity played in limiting my choices—a dynamic that would exert itself repeatedly over the coming years, with heartbreaking results.

At Boston College Clara often attended races with my parents and her father to watch me compete. She loved being around people, and the team loved her. I remember one day spotting her, still in diapers, walking among the trees near the end of the course, her little head tilted as she took in the roots of the trees and the runners surrounding her. After the race, I scooped her up, the familiar padding of her "diapied" behind resting on my arm. Holding her close was the sweetest feeling in the world, as we shared the joy and excitement of the moment, together, each for our own reason.

I graduated in 1996—a 22-year-old with a 3.67 GPA and a toe-headed toddler on my hip.

The Three of Us

We travel together, passengers on a little spaceship,
dependent on its vulnerable reserves of air and soil,
all committed, for our safety, to its security and peace.
Preserved from annihilation only by the care,
the work and the love we give our fragile craft.

Adlai E. Stevenson II
American Lawyer, Politician, and Diplomat

The winter after I finished my degree, Cal, Clara and I moved to Princeton, where Cal was still working on his undergraduate degree. We left our families behind and moved into our first apartment together on campus. Clara was two years old.

We arrived on a dark night in January 1997 with a lot of possessions, including the running stroller, to move up the stairs into our new home in the Princeton University faculty housing, where other families resided. I remember my little baby girl transitioning from her crib to a bed in this apartment. As we settled in, I would sometimes break down in tears at the thought of my baby growing up. The more aware she became, the more I saw our life through her eyes and worried about making the best choices for her.

That spring, in 1997, Cal graduated summa cum laude with his degree in economics, and Clara had developed a prodigious vocabulary. At his graduation, she waited for him after the ceremony to say proudly, "Congraduwations on your gradwuation, Daddy!"

That summer, I used some money my grandmother had left me when she passed away to take the three of us on a trip to Europe. I had always hoped to one day live in Spain, and now I wanted to seize the opportunity for our young family to go overseas before Cal and I settled into a more permanent life.

It should have been fun putting the trip together, but making even the smallest decision was hell, with Cal trying to control every detail from planning to packing. My sister had given me some small toys to keep Clara entertained on the flight but, with little explanation or warning, he threw them into a garbage bin at the airport.

Since my years at Boston College, when we'd had the constant help of family, he had gotten better at controlling his tantrums but his need to assert psychological control over me and Clara seemed to be getting worse. In Europe, we had a disagreement that left me with a fist-sized bruise on my arm.

Cal was rough with our daughter, too. He had a habit of picking her up by one arm. Time and time again, I pleaded, "Please don't pick her up like that. It hurts her."

"If you can find it in a book somewhere or get a professional to tell me that I should not pick her up by her arm, then I will stop," he argued.

I did. And he did. Well, for the most part. Cal's insistence that I find another opinion on his actions is a form of psychological manipulation called triangulation. Triangulation weakens any arguments that go against the aim of the abusive partner to control a situation. It is a sophisticated form of intimate partner bullying and incredibly effective at tearing down a person's self-worth.

Running

At Princeton University, we lived in faculty housing on campus, near a little bridge over a waterway the rowing crew used to practice on. I cherished every chance I got to go running around the beautiful campus grounds. I'd take my blonde, curly-haired daughter out in the running stroller and lope along behind her for miles. I had been reading her the story of Three Billy Goats Gruff, in which three Billy goats cross a bridge, outwitting a troll who wants to capture them! On our way home, I would push my daughter back and forth across the little bridge, over and over, repeating the line from the story, "Who is that running over my bridge?" She would giggle wildly every time! Eventually, we'd evade the troll who was out to get us and run off the bridge together to safety, across the perfectly groomed, endless Princeton green.

Trying

Josephine is ferocious and strong like a wolverine! What an accomplishment for an American to complete the Vasaloppet.

Janne Stefansson
Seven-time winner of the Vasaloppet

After returning from Europe, in the summer of 1997, we settled down in Norwalk, Connecticut, near where Cal had found a job, about a three-hour drive from our families. Our new apartment was covered in a film of grime and required a lot of cleaning. The rent was high for us. I was caring for our not-yet-three-year-old child and working three part-time jobs that accommodated our schedules. Every day it became clearer what a bright child we had, with an endless capacity for learning—and a great memory.

Years later, Clara would recount one summer evening in her running stroller. I was surprised when she began to talk about what had happened, though it was something I had never forgotten. Cal was pushing the stroller, while I jogged alongside, when he began to give it a hard push ahead then run to catch up. With each push, the distance got wider and wider, until all I could see in my mind's eye was a car backing up or the stroller tipping over.

I screamed at him, "Stop that! She's going to get hurt!"

As often happened, my pleas only served to egg him on. He

let the stroller go down the steepest hill in town. I could barely catch up. When I finally got a hold of it, I didn't let go.

When I told a friend about this incident, she dismissed it as "The way guys are . . . They're just rougher with kids is all."

Cal's harsh behaviors were psychologically abusive. Psychological abuse is often the most sadistic form of abuse, carried out with a sophisticated process and with great deliberateness. Emotionally or psychologically abusive traits include but are not limited to causing fear by threatening physical harm to self, partner, and children.

Clara started pre-school a few months after we settled in Connecticut. She immediately made a friend named Katie. She asked me if we could play with Katie sometime. Desperate for friendship myself, I called Katie's mom to make a play date.

We met on a sunny day at the beach in Rowayton. I handed Katie an apple, assuring her mom, "It's organic. You don't have to wash it." She laughed, saying she was sure Katie would survive. By the time the sun had started to go down, she'd invited me to join a women's Bible study group that met at her house.

The group of women I encountered there was a salve to my hurting soul. They were kind and nurturing. As a young couple with a child, new jobs, and a new apartment in a new town, Cal and I were in the process of a major transition. This group would help to see me through the transition, and become more grounded.

Through my part-time jobs, some babysitting that I'd taken on, the Bible study group, and my new running community, I began to make friends in town. My new network led me to be hired on by a broker at a well-known investment firm. It was a privilege to work for one of the top producers in the country for a little over a year and a half, earning close to what Cal was making.

Simultaneously, my faith was deepening as I witnessed what felt like peace and truth in the lives of the women in my bible study group. There was something tangible to hold onto. As I got to know their families, I found myself wanting what they all seemed to have: a peaceful home and a life partner.

I told Cal that I was ready to commit to him in marriage.

Clara and I began attending the Lutheran church that my friends from the study group attended, and Cal reluctantly joined us. Now that I understood the direction I wanted to take, life began to feel more stable. I wanted to bring closure to my rickety old relationship with my boyfriend and make a solid family for my child with a commitment to her father. I was witnessing in my friends how to make this a reality, and it all made more sense to me than what I had known before in my young adult life.

One evening in October of 1998, with roses and champagne and a roaring fire in the fireplace, Cal asked me to marry him. We were 23 and 24 years old. Clara was just shy of her 4th birthday. I believed that through the power of the Holy Spirit we could overcome our challenges and heal the past wounds. I was so thankful that my home would now be complete and confident. The years of hard work, schooling, relocating, and adjusting had finally led us to solid ground.

We would become Mr. and Mrs. Cal Bering in 10 months, and I had one thing I absolutely had to accomplish before settling into married life—ski the Vasaloppet. I had started training during the summer of 1998. I had adjusted my diet and was preparing for this big race that I had dreamed of, to complete it in February 1999.

XC Skiing and the Vasaloppet

My mom had introduced me to her Swedish friend Rayna when I was pregnant with Clara, for the purposes of teaching me prenatal yoga. It was through this friendship that I became enthralled with the idea of skiing the Vasaloppet—a cross-country ski event in Sweden that traverses the 90 kilometers between Sälen and Mora.

As Rayna spoke of checkpoints where they served blueberry soup and blood pudding with lingonberry jelly, my mind wandered to the terrain. When she told me about the high level of camaraderie and enthusiasm among the athletes, I thought about the physical challenge. I knew I had to try to ski it someday.

Three years later, after months of training, I was on a plane to Sweden with Rayna and my mother. It was February 1999. Cal and I had just gotten engaged in the fall. I figured this would be my one last big adventure before we married and started to add to our family.

When we arrived in Sweden, my stomach hurt so bad I could barely function. I went to the doctor, who could find nothing wrong. "Nerves," he said. He'd seen it before, he added, "at Vasaloppet time." After a lifetime of competitive running, plus recent cross-country ski racing in Vermont, I could hardly believe it. Then again, I had been building this race up in my head for years.

I had all the gear, too, including a "Freshette"—a funnel used by women skiers to pee with their pants up. (I regretted not practicing with it more before the race, as I was so clumsy with

33

it I may as well have just kept skiing and peed my pants.)

The Vasaloppet has two course options: 25K and 90K. I chose the 90K.

Up until this race, good quality gear had been something other people had. But I was ready this time—polyester everything, the right kind of vest, the freshette. I cut up Power Bars into bite-sized pieces so I could suck on them if they froze and wore a camel pack filled with Gatorade. It was 1998 and I was finally geared up properly—this was a far cry from my 6th grade Keds run!

We started in a vast open field that led to a narrower trail up a hill. It was the most congested the race was ever going to be. The first skier to pass me was wearing faded, holey blue jeans, a plaid flannel shirt, and wool mittens. The Keds version of ski gear.

Rayna waited for me at each checkpoint to be sure I was ok— given she is 25 years my senior, this was more than a little humbling. It had not been possible to train in the states for Vasaloppet's conditions. There was no snow in Connecticut, so I'd trained by running around Waveny Park with ski poles and boots, mimicking the movement of classic skiing. I wasn't sophisticated enough to have the roller skis. Mostly, I wasn't prepared for the cold. By the time I hit the five-hour mark, I had reached what would have been my maximum exposure time back home—and, at seven and a half hours, I wasn't halfway through the race. At the 45K mark, I was overcome with nausea and a headache. None of my supplies tasted palatable. My stiff, heavy legs threatened to quit. I felt like the tin man with morning sickness. My knees were stiff and the fibers of my quadriceps maxed out, dried up.

The normally welcome down-hills only worsened my nausea. Even the slightest touch of wind on my forehead exacerbated the ache behind my skull—an ache that seemed to connect directly to my stomach, where it would trigger another wave of nausea.

By the time evening had given way to the night sky and the tall black trees stood outlined against the bright stars, snowmobiles had begun to show up along the course, picking up the stragglers. Waiting for me at a checkpoint, Rayna informed me I had only one more checkpoint to go through. I advised her to go on ahead of me. It was obvious she had the wherewithal to complete the race, while the door was closing on me. As a competitor, I was uncomfortably aware of how important it is to "ski your own race." Reluctantly, but obviously relieved, she skied on ahead.

Now, we each had our own race to ski.

I trudged ahead—lifeless, defeated. I thought to myself, I've been planning this race for four years—I can't believe it's going to end this way. The blueberry soup and lingonberry jelly at the checkpoints were the only part of this dream that seemed destined to come true for me.

A snow machine pulled up next to me and the driver asked if I thought I should keep going.

I said, "Well, I'm kind of bummed out, because I don't want to give up. But I don't think I'll make it in time through the last check point."

He shouted back, "You have only 800 yards to go! And five minutes to get there!" His words lit a fire under me. A half mile doesn't take five minutes, I thought. I began to ski hard. Motoring along next to me, my rescuer must have been very surprised as my death march broke into a sprint. I made it to the last checkpoint and kept going. I skied without thinking now. Up a slight hill, rounding a corner...

Are my eyes deceiving me? What are those bright lights? The finish line?

I had been out for 12 hours but came barreling down that final stretch as if it were the finish of a 5K. I then heard my name *announced over the loud speakers, as I had heard it announced so many times before. Only, this time, I had completed the Vasaloppet.*

My mom was waiting with Rayna at the finish line. "Mom," I panted, as I fell into her arms, "that was harder than labor."

I got up early the next morning to go on a 5K ski with Rayna. Our host and multiple-year Vasaloppet winner, Janne Stefansson, stopped us as we were heading out the door.

"She's a wolverine," he said to Rayna in Swedish. She later explained to me this was a high compliment—at that time, unbeknown to me, not many Americans had completed the Vasaloppet.

Locating and Relocating

The well-being of others is at stake with secrecy.

Josephine May

In the summer of 2000, almost one year after we were married, I left my job at the brokerage firm in Greenwich and Cal left the company he'd been working for in Darien, and we moved to rural western New Hampshire. We purchased an 1880s farmhouse. A quaint and tiny home on an acre of land surrounded by farms. Our plan from here forward was that I would raise the children and Cal would support the family. Our second child and first bouncing baby boy, Andrew, was born in June of 2001, just before our second wedding anniversary.

Having more children was a dream of mine. I had always wanted to be a wife and a mother. Parenting was a challenge and Andrew was very clingy to me. He rarely wanted to be with Cal. Andrew cried a lot as a baby. He always wanted me to hold him and he had difficulty getting settled. This was challenging enough on its own and then there was this guilt of how to parent Clara while trying to console Andrew, and Cal.

Andrew wasn't yet even a year old when, one night as we were sitting at the table, his father handed him a potato right out of the oven. Andrew immediately howled in pain.

"Why would you do that?!" I asked incredulously.

"I wanted to see his reaction."

I was irate, shocked and confused by his lack of sensitivity to our little child.

"You don't hand a baby a hot potato! Of course he's going to take it from you. He trusts you!" *Or he did*, I thought. Cal had no reaction to my comments. It was as if I didn't exist and my concern was of no interest to him.

I felt suffocated, but I went on as a mother who wanted peace for her home. I didn't know it, but I was being groomed to understand that I was insignificant. Over time, like the frog in the boiling pot of water, I would be brainwashed to believe that the only opinion that mattered was Cal's; the whole family was conditioned to believe that only his opinion mattered. Thus, the seeds were deeply sown for isolation and triangulation.

Frequently moving for new employment opportunities, to prevent us from setting up a support system, Cal implemented a common pattern of abusive isolation. Moving frequently creates isolation, chaos, and dependency on the abuser. It also conceals behaviors from extended family that might be otherwise questioned. Isolation is the first step in convincing a victim that their controller is the most important person in their life. The reason why abusers isolate their victims from friends and family is that abuse is about control and victims are more easily controlled mentally and physically when they don't have trusted confidants to turn to. Cal had my trust that he would do what was right for our family, which fit well into his job selections, constantly moving us away from family and friends. I wanted to be near my family but we were always a long road trip away.

Also in effect here was triangulation. Triangulation is a complex abuse tactic that can also involve pitting two people against each other, controlling the information that is shared between the two parties, and thus providing power to the abuser as the primary contact person and the conduit of information. By disempowering me and empowering Clara, Cal was setting both of us up for abuse and isolation. Clara would be taught to believe that I was incompetent and not a person she could confide in or ask for help. I would see Clara and Cal as having a strong father-daughter bond that would protect and promote her in the future, therefore I would sideline myself in order to ensure that Clara was absorbing all that she needed to engender strength and empowerment for her life. Cal would control the image and the communication so that it benefitted him. He capitalized on my desire to promote Clara and he also capitalized on Clara's innocence.

Children are wired for survival and therefore seek the refuge of the perceived stronger parent. In a sexually abusive situation, the abuser intentionally creates this unhealthy power dynamic using triangulation, because it leaves the children believing that they have no one to turn to for help. Developmentally, children lack the capacity to determine that it is inappropriate for their father to elevate them to an authoritative status above their mother. They don't want that level of power because it scares them, but they don't want to let it go because it aligns them with the authority figure in the home. Triangulation is damaging to the entire family unit and each member of the family is adversely affected by this dynamic because it creates instability.

In an article from the Open Minds Foundation titled *Larry Nassar: the Pedophile Who Groomed Hundreds*, the editorial staff offers the following explanation of how grooming and triangulation work, and why we must be aware of it these dynamics:

"Pedophile grooming relies on a confidence trick, just like any phone scam or pyramid scheme; it trades on the innocence of children rather than money, but the traps a predator uses to lure victims into danger, and the web of undue influence they weave to keep their victims ensnared, remain the same. If we are to break the cycle of sex abuse scandals rocking even our most venerable institutions, we must educate children, parents, judges, police, lawyers, mental health professionals and everyone involved to recognize the patterns of abuse—and not to repeat yesterday's mistakes in failing to use our healthy skepticism. Only when we face grooming for what it is can we keep our children safe."

When Clara was young, I didn't know what grooming was. The predatory traps that Cal was using to keep us ensnared were chipping away at our integrity, methodically and yet invisibly. Wearing down my self-esteem by devaluing my opinions, secretly undermining our family by sexually abusing his daughter; Cal made it clear that his opinion was the only option. It was an exhausting and futile process trying to communicate my needs and the children's needs to him; he had no concern for us.

In an attempt to establish a peaceful home life, I began to homeschool Clara in the fall of 2001. The idea of homeschooling was one that I suggested, and Cal quickly supported by implementing an immediate purchase of curriculum and supplies. This was a decision I wholeheartedly regret. Homeschooling Clara from first through eighth grade lead to further isolation, heightened pressure on me with academic expectations and a finish line that was always out of reach for both of us.

While I was working to forge a stronger "we," Cal seemed more focused than ever on his own needs. When he did agree to counseling, I found myself fighting to suppress the messages embedded in the things he was saying. He made it clear to the therapist that, while he considered our children to be his top priority, he felt I could fend for myself and had no right to expect much from him. I so acclimated to this abject treatment that I accepted it. He was who I married, and I adjusted my expectations to what he could give emotionally.

Two years after the birth of our beautiful, healthy boy we said goodbye to our quaint farmhouse, the apricot tree my mom had planted to commemorate Andrew's birth, the woodpile for our wood stove, Mr. Borden's raspberry and blueberry farm and his maple syrup shack, the sledding hill behind our house that had been the scene of so many fun winter gatherings, the cross-country skiing I'd enjoyed all around the vast wooded surrounding farms, and the ponds we swam in during the summers. We said goodbye to our friends, many of them young parents, too, and our daughter said goodbye to the good friends she'd made in New Hampshire.

Cal accepted a job working for Bowdoin College, moving us to Brunswick, Maine. He found a spacious beach house in Harpswell for us to rent before purchasing a charming cape-style home adjacent to the college campus.

We built a sweet church community, and loved sharing occasions with our neighbors, but our time there would be short-lived, too.

One day I heard him come home early, walk through the front door, and climb the steps to our bedroom, which I was busy painting a grayish-lavender color. Standing in the doorway in his khaki pants, gingham shirt, and trademark wild hair, he said to me, "You'd better start looking for a job." Cal lost his job after only nine months. It was the summer of 2003. We were looking at yet another move.

I sat there with paintbrush in hand, feeling guilty for the

stress that he had been under and the relationship that he had with his boss, where he reported that she treated him terribly. I went to work at a doctor's office over the summer while Cal took care of the kids and looked for work.

Cal's losing his job had followed a period of difficult communication and conflict in our home life. We were now in our mid-20s with two children; even though we were still young, our strained history seemed to stretch back over an eternity. With the understanding that every couple faces challenges in marriage, I naively believed that we struggled with the same kind of issues.

Even with my commitment to our marriage and my faith in God, I was becoming concerned with our years of not being able to connect and cooperate on even a basic level. Day after day, Cal had come home from work and launched into some tirade. He was endlessly angry and accusatory: dissatisfied with the dinner I'd prepared, upset that the baby was crying or unhappy with my homeschool curriculum and the standards I set for Clara.

Though I had taken it on myself to be a good, kind wife and homemaker, my husband consistently minimized my efforts. His antagonistic, belittling words dominated the soundtrack to our marriage. It was becoming impossible not to acknowledge that I was on a never-ending treadmill, trying to improve and not experiencing any warmth or consideration from my spouse in return.

When we first moved into the rental home in Harpswell, I suggested we split up. Cal pleaded for us to go away together— just the two of us without the stress of the kids. His sister was graduating from a master's program, and we would have time to just be together to celebrate her graduation and cut loose a little. "When the vacation is over," he said, "if you still feel this way, we can begin the divorce process."

The vacation provided a few days away from parenting concerns. Being in a new environment with Cal's family, celebrating his sister's achievement, and dancing out in the city were fun things that gave me hope and got me back on board. I had just needed to know that life with Cal could have moments of fun and joy. My greatest desire in life remained for us to be a loving and united household—a place our children would long to come home to, where our family would blossom. This vision and my faith kept me in the fight for my marriage.

One day when we were walking across the baseball field, Cal playfully picked up Clara, who was 8 years old, and carried her a few feet like a princess and then suddenly dropped her flat on her back. She looked up at him in shock: "I never thought you would do that," she sobbed.

I looked on in horror as this sweet, loving little girl lay shocked and humiliated on the baseball field. I reached for her but no matter how much love I offered, her heart was broken because her daddy was reminding her that she was never secure with him and her mother was powerless to take her pain away.

"Cal! Oh my goodness! How could you think that was funny?!" I exclaimed as I reached to comfort her while he laughed at us.

These behaviors always came as such a shock that I didn't know where to begin in getting him to stop. He appeared to care little about any harm he caused to the kids and even less about what I might have to say about it. Yet I had come to chalk up these events to mere insensitivity, unable to accept that he would intentionally hurt us. I started over every day, renewing my faith that both our spirits would begin to seek grounding.

I longed for a community to raise our children in, where we could develop long-term friendships. I assumed Cal wanted this, too. After months of searching, Cal finally had a job offer in the fall of 2003 and we flew to Alaska to confirm our next adventure.

I knew that relocating so far away from my family was not without risk, but I was also still very young, strong, and adventurous. I had faith in Cal's ability to provide and my ability to build a community for our family. My faith kept alive the hope and dream that our family could thrive and overcome our obstacles. Maybe an extreme move would jolt us out of our old patterns. For me, I could not understand that the only way to change "our old patterns" was to leave the relationship. Cal sat back and enjoyed my efforts, the security of my devotion to our marriage, and my willingness to try to change; all while he lived exactly as he pleased and exploited my desire to grow together as a family.

Running

I adored my new home and neighborhood in Brunswick, Maine. My daily run, sometimes included jogging down our lovely avenue where the neighbor's homes offered an array of well-maintained flower gardens. Such beauty always caused me to pause and observe the unique shapes, colors, and fresh new fragrances. If I took the path through my backyard which abutted the baseball field, there I would encounter soft turf gently making grassy mud imprints under my feet and enjoy the smell of the cool grass filling my senses. Our two-year-old yellow lab, Sparky, playfully chased his tennis ball while he ran with me, until I dropped him off on our back porch for a cold drink of water, and headed down to the field house to do some speed work on the indoor track. The track was a place where I could return to my core, my essence, and tune out the world. On occasion, the fieldhouse was also a location that I had the fortune of crossing paths with my childhood hero, Joan Benoit-Samuelson.

Alaska

We need to constantly re-examine our culture.
What does respect mean?
What is sacrifice?
What's cooperation?
If you expect people to respect you, you have to respect yourself,
respect your conduct and others will respect you.

Walter Soboleff
Alaska Native icon

How long will we be here? There is a massive blue glacier outside my garage door surrounded by towering mountain peaks. The air smells different, cleaner and sweeter. The tap water is pure. Tall pine trees line the neighborhoods. Boats are parked in driveways or on lawns. The roofs on the houses are made of different material because of all the rain. The buildings are shorter and boxier. The newspaper looks like a science magazine with pictures of wildlife. People eat King crab or Dungeness crab—not lobster. The devil's club leaves are so enormous that they look prehistoric. There are thimble berries and salmon berries in addition to blueberries and raspberries. Day light lasts all day in the summer, and long, dark days mark the winter. Bears running through my front yard, hop the fence. Neighbors fasten my garbage cans shut with bungie cords to keep the ravens out. It takes longer to ski down the mountain than it does to wait in line for the chair lift. This is a different world.

After a little over 2 years in Alaska, in March of 2006, we welcomed our third child, Jason. Clara was 11 years old when Jason was born, and Andrew was 4.5 years old.

During my pregnancy, Cal paid even less attention to me than usual.

"Why don't you ever try to be close to me?" I asked.

"I don't find you attractive," he responded coldly. His words shattered me, not because I believed I was an unattractive woman, but because I knew how mean my husband had to be to speak to me that way. I left the house and took a long walk to the glacier. Looking out over its blue ice, I once again reconciled myself to the fact that I was ever more alone in this relationship.

Later, I mentioned the conversation to a family member, who said, "Maybe he meant he just wasn't attracted to you during your pregnancy." This still didn't sit right with me. I began to suspect the problem was something else, something deeper. But I just could not for the life of me give words to the coldness, the lack of humanness that I felt in his presence. I used to say to him that being around him was like sucking on a lollipop with the wrapper still on. There was no life, no flavor, no reaction, no communication or sharing.

My three children were as beautiful and sweet as my husband was distant and cruel.

At three years old, in 2009, Jason was ready for potty training. His potty training got on his father's nerves even worse than Clara's had. When he had the inevitable accident, Cal impulsively snatched him up by the arm and spanked his tender little body as hard as he could.

"You cannot beat a child who is potty training," I pleaded. "He is just learning how to use the toilet. That is the stuff that causes all kinds of problems later in life. Don't hit him! You hit him so hard for having an accident!"

He looked away from me, muttering flatly, "Sorry."

"Apologize to Jason," I insisted.

He then apologized to our baby son. Nothing he said could remedy the confusion both Jason and I were feeling over his violent outburst. Cal didn't really seem to notice Jason most of the time. Jason was an easy baby and I adored him. Even though Jason was born via cesarean section and I feared that this would decrease our connection, I felt strongly connected to him as an infant and a toddler.

Cal's mannerisms finally tipped me over the edge from thinking it was me and I began to study his behavior. At first I studied him to better understand how to be in a relationship with him; later I studied Cal's behaviors to educate myself on the antisocial personality disorders known as the dark triad that Cal was presenting through his interactions with our family: psychopathy, narcissism, and Machiavellianism.

Cal doesn't have empathy or humane behaviors. People's lives are not important to him. Control is what Cal thrives on. When he saw how close I was with my children, with Jason, he sought to destroy that closeness and any potential for our lifelong connection. He couldn't stand to witness that closeness because he is incapable of it.

Some of Cal's behaviors were subtle and more difficult to label. He would be inappropriately sarcastic with the little kids, who couldn't understand him. Where most parents would know that young children can't process sarcasm and find it hurtful, Cal wasn't concerned about how his attitude or comments or teaching impacted the children.

When we moved to Alaska, Cal and I had the opportunity to purchase a home in a fun neighborhood with lots of kids and families for us to socialize with. It was slightly out of our reach financially, but if I worked part-time, we could easily have afforded this home which would have been a good investment and a fun place to live. Cal wouldn't hear of it.

"I'm afraid that my coworkers will view us as elitist if we buy that home. I don't want to start off on the wrong foot."

"I could work part time during the evenings and we could easily afford this mortgage payment."

"No. It's a small town and I think it's important that we live a humble lifestyle. We are going to purchase the attached home and we can upgrade if my income allows."

"Cal, we're only talking about a twenty-thousand-dollar difference. I can easily make that up if I get a job, and I know we'll be happier in a more social environment."

We purchased the attached home. I went to work painting the small, plain interior. It was a fine transition home but it lacked the much needed instant community we might have had if my input had been considered. The layout was a large common room with vaulted ceilings that included the kitchen and living room. A long hallway off which were two bedrooms and a garage all facing the glacier.

The entire family was always in close proximity. We sat at the dining room table with Clara for homeschooling. Andrew was just a toddler when we first moved into this home, and there were constant distractions.

"Daddy, I read the Saxon math chapters that you assigned to me, I promise," said Clara as she sat at the dining room table, anxious about Cal's dissatisfied demeanor and intimidating, belittling comments.

"You haven't done any of the worksheets that I've assigned to you Clara! What could be so hard about this math? If you read the assignment, how could you not understand the material?! Are you an idiot?!"

"Daddy, I don't know why I don't know how to do the math." Her voice quivered. "I'll try harder. I've been taking care of Andrew a lot. It's distracting."

"You are pathetic. There is no reason why you could not get this work done, unless you're an idiot. I don't want to hear your lame excuses. I've already explained this to you. You don't get your work done because you're lazy. You have five worksheets to do by the morning; if they are not done, I will double the assignment and you will not go to youth group."

Nine-year-old Clara sat at the dinner table in her little yellow pastel turtleneck shirt, tears pouring down her soft cheeks as he kept piling on math problem after math problem, offering little or no instruction.

"Daddy, I just don't understand the math."

"What don't you understand? I just told you this! You are not listening!"

I tried to step in.

"Cal. There is no way she can learn under the amount of stress you are creating right now. She's tuned you out because you are scaring her."

"Maybe she needs to be scared. She's not getting any work done."

"Mom, don't. You will just make things worse."

Cal had an insane look in his eyes and Clara knew as well as I, we were going to end up arguing in front of her and the boys, and that *would* only make things worse. My husband's torture was a subtle no-win chess game with rules that constantly changed to keep him in power.

One of Clara's few social outlets was her youth group. She would get so excited leading up to one of their planned outings, longing for the freedom of being with her friends, and away from home. Cal usually let her go, but he routinely stalled so long she would be late to rendezvous with her friends. I never understood the abnormal psychology behind it, but I knew he was intentionally trying to frustrate her so that she would show up angry or out of sorts.

For me, it was so important to instill in my children and myself a sense of community and love, like the family that I grew up in. I hosted family friends and a mother's group on a regular basis. In conversations with my women friends, we discussed our marriages, and I confessed that I was at a loss to know how to make mine better. Everyone talked about how difficult marriage was. Our families all had things in common—hunting trips, planning meals and child care, managing and keeping up our homes, etc. But I suspected that *my* family's issues were more serious than any of my friends'. I just didn't yet know what was wrong.

I turned to the self-help industry, studying various love languages, personality types, parenting books, marriage books, and philosophers from Eckhart Tolle to Thomas Merton. I tried keeping the house cleaner and our lives more organized. I only spent money on groceries, trying to make a home like the one I'd grown up in, filled with food and people. My shelves were stuffed with books on how to improve myself and my household. I tried it all, yet the truth remained that I could do nothing to make my home a less tense place. Later, I would learn that Cal had deliberately set up our family to fear his moods and set me up to constantly strive to placate him. He kept me so busy trying to keep the peace, I had no time to contemplate the harm he may have been causing our children or to improve myself professionally.

Andrew and Jason were super sweet, but somehow managed to easily exasperate Cal.

"You will obey me! You hurt your little brother on purpose," he growled, pinning Andrew against the living room wall. Andrew's body dangled high above Cal's head, as Cal shouted up into Andrew's face.

Terrified, Andrew just stared into the angry eyes of his father. He was seven years old and his two-year-old brother was annoying him. Cal would have him know that it was not okay for Andrew to be annoyed. He expected him to care for his little brother and protect him.

There is never a circumstance that warrants pinning the kid to the wall and shouting in his face. I felt like I was going to throw-up.

What Cal did to Andrew in this instance was give him the message that he owned him. Andrew was not to be a kid, he was to be a mature care-giver to his two-year-old brother. If he didn't do as Cal demanded, he could not be sure of what the reaction might be. The inconsistency and fear created anxiety and loss of personal worth for Andrew.

"Andrew. Did you eat all of your lunch yesterday?" Cal would start in on him at the dinner table as we all sat around for a meal.

"Daddy, I don't remember."

"You didn't. Get up and go to your room."

"Cal, what are you doing?!"

"Josephine, he's wasting food."

"He's seven years old! You are bringing up yesterday's meal. This is crazy. Andrew, come with me. I'll read to you in your room."

Holding my hand as we walked off to his room together he looked up at me with tear-filled brown eyes.

"Mom, what did I do wrong?"

"Nothing Andrew. Daddy is just cranky right now."

Cal turned on us for reasons impossible to identify, leaving us in a maelstrom of emotions that we were at a loss to know what to do with. The above incident was a common experience for Andrew. Cal is a textbook narcissistic parent. He implemented every single strategy used by a narcissistic parent and assigned each child in our household with a role. This process is clearly described in an article found in the *Huffington Post* titled "The Narcissistic Parent's Psychological Warfare: Parentifying, Idealizing, and Scapegoating." The narcissist parent assigns roles to his children to meet his emotional needs and pit family members against one another. Typically, there is a golden child and one or more scapegoats. Golden children are idealized, while scapegoats are devalued and even neglected or disowned.

The kids turned their attention outward, getting involved in endless activities like soccer, skiing, swimming, theatre, music lessons, and youth groups. We homeschooled for years, and the homeschool group, an extension of our church community, came to occupy a central place in our lives.

There were times when Cal would be involved in the children's lives and seem to do well with them. He developed friendships with his co-workers and exchanged ideas about what ski gear to buy for the kids, vacations and trips, investments, and purchases. His social circle was small but, at these times, he seemed to enjoy work and spending time with the family.

From what I heard and understood, he was respected at work. I used to say, "Don't use up all of your nice behavior at work and then come home and treat us like dirt." He worked with an intelligent group of men and women. He was closest to his boss, who came from a big Midwestern Catholic family. His boss' wife ran in social circles that I passed through on occasion. Since both our families had moved to Alaska from other communities, we began spending holidays, birthdays, and work events together. Skiing and ski team brought us closer, too. I brought other friends and a life of faith into our home, and it seemed like we were achieving a bit more balance during our first years in Alaska.

While Cal's and my friendships were cordial, they were still somewhat distant. One friend from Cal's office told me that Cal frequently mentioned that I was always unhappy and difficult to please.

At the time, I never understood the random patterns of care my husband provided for me and the children. Our home was nice, but he made a really big deal if I wanted to buy silverware or curtains. Yet, when his sister and her fiancé were coming up for a visit, he made the unilateral decision to run out and purchase new furniture.

"It seems like you take offense at the mention of improving our home or our future," I said, as we crammed two car seats and a teenager in the back of our 5 passenger vehicle, loaded with ski equipment.

"You just want to be like your sisters. I'm not into keeping up with the Joneses. Maybe you should just be happy with what you have," Cal bitterly responded.

"I am happy with what I have but I don't feel the freedom to talk about plans or dreams for our future," I gently responded, trying to navigate Cal's palpable hostility.

He immobilized the family with tension and anger. Instead of battling with him to be heard, which only hurt my children by creating more tension and anger in the house, I stopped looking to him for the kind of close companionship and friendship that I had once desired in a marriage. This internalization of his cold responses became detrimental to my self-esteem. My expectations of love, joy, hope, fun and growth were diminished. This still impacts me today socially, because I absorbed his message of my lack of value so profoundly that I eventually could not see my own worth in social settings.

I did my best to anticipate his needs and give him plenty of room, for sleep, alone time, social time, athletics, boys' nights out, hunting, and tinkering around the house. I endeavored to help him get what he needed to be happy and successful.

When I turned 35, it dawned on me that I rarely did anything for myself. I decided that I wanted to teach yoga. I had heard of a program that was being offered in Arizona called "Holy Yoga," which would combine my Christian faith with my athleticism. When I raised the idea of going to this training, Cal emphatically clamped down on the idea and fought me on participating. For once, I just said, "I'm doing this."

He was worried about cost. I was worried about leaving my children alone with their father. By this time, Clara was 14 and had been taking on a lot of the responsibility of caring for her younger siblings. I trusted her but felt terrible about leaving her and the other children with their erratic father, so I had never before dared to leave.

When I called home from Arizona to check in, Clara was busy caring for the family. Her voice sounded flat and I knew she was resigned to the burden of childcare and a hostile home environment. I had left her no choice. It was so painful to know that, because my husband was so inconsiderate, the only way I could gain a modicum of freedom for myself was to take it from her. In a normal home, she would simply have been helping her dad while Mom was away. In our home, as I would later discover, we were all being manipulated to an abusive end.

I called my father and cried. "Dad, something is not right with my husband. I don't know what it is, but it's so stressful. I need help. Can you help me?"

"Yes," he promised. I'm sure everything in him wanted to help me, but the reality is he could not have fixed my situation.

To the inexperienced eye, it looked like my parents and siblings just went on with their lives. But really, they did not know how to help. No one, not my family, not Cal's co-workers, neither our church nor community—and, ultimately, the legal system—could understand what we were dealing with.

My time away at Holy Yoga marked an awakening to life without being coerced or controlled. For the first time in my adult life, I had gotten away from Cal for a whole week, and it changed me. Instead of trying to figure out what I could change about myself to make our home-life better, I started reading about and applying boundaries.

So much came to light in my short time away from Cal. His abuse and control were subtle and constant, but the relief that came with suddenly removing him from my daily life was instantaneous, like coming out of a trance. I could see. I could breathe. I could feel. My emotions were honored and considered by the people around me. Being so unaccustomed to having an adult listen to me, the contrast of this week-long retreat stirred and confused me as I experienced genuine caring interactions.

Bear Spray

Clara is eleven years old and she has dubbed our family outings as "D.A.D." hikes, (Disastrous And Dangerous). She declines the family outing, so we head out to the Glacier Trail with six-month-old baby Jason, and five-year-old Andrew. My husband is riding his bike, towing our two small children behind him in the bike trailer.

Running along beside the kids, my eyes are intensely scanning the baby trailer hitting roots and bumping over the tricky terrain. Before my reach can prevent calamity, the trailer tire catches the edge of a stump, flipping the trailer over. The adrenaline already pumping through my hormonal body surges. As the kids launch from the carriage, Andrew instinctively wraps himself around his baby brother, protecting Jason's fragile body from taking the impact of the jutting roots and jagged rocks protruding from the forest floor.

Seeing that the kids are not badly injured, we collect ourselves and make our way further down the wooded path. Finally, we arrive at the sandy embankment at the end of the trail, along-side of the glacial stream. As I unpack our snacks, I hear a rustle in the bushes... "Wait, shhh. I think I hear something."

My husband pops the pin out of the bear spray canister and hikes into the bushes looking for a bear. When he comes back alone we all breathe a sigh of relief. Cal puts the canister back in his pocket and traverses through the cold glacial water with Andrew, onto a patch of silt and sand. It's a warm, sunny, gorgeous day in Alaska. My gaze drifts to the spectacular sight of the glacier as I dreamily sit on the other side of the cold, rushing water, nursing Jason. Peaceful, and safe from the so-called bear in the woods, I happily hold my baby and watch my young son and his dad play in nature. Cal puts Andrew on his shoulders because his little feet are cold. With my son on his shoulders, he squats down to pick up a curiosity and I hear a "TSSSSST" noise. I watch as my husband's eyes grow as wide as saucers.   He hastily sets Andrew down. Again, I hear, "TSSSSSSSSSSST."

The next thing I witness are Cal's tan hiking shorts on the ground and he's squatting in the water with a panic. He emerges from the water and for a moment I quizzically look at his tighty-whities covered in an explosion of bright autumn orange. The bear spray?!

Immediately, the field nurse within me awakens. I hand my husband a clump of cold silt to put on his package, thinking that it would draw the potent spray out of his skin, as if I was treating a bee sting. He opts for the glacial water after my mudpack fails to offer any relief. He then begins the 4-mile return trek, bobbing in and out of the glacial water stream, intermittently seeking comfort for his fire-b***s in the icy-cold water.

Quickly, I convert the trailer into a running stroller, tuck the kids in, and stash the bike behind some trees. I run us out of the woods to the parking lot where Cal is waiting, doubled over next to the Subaru, wearing my pink running shorts. Kids and bear-sprayed b***s land in the car.

The ranger station is nearby. The rangers probably have an antidote. With urgency, I pull up to the forest service station and jump out of the Subaru to find a remedy for my husband's bear spray covered b***s. Inside, the ranger doesn't flinch as I convey the mishap. Barely looking at me, he lackadaisically responds to my panic with a very s-l-o-w: "It happens." I usher the ranger outside to find Cal at the side of the station, with a garden hose funneled through his shorts and hyperventilating from the pain. The ranger reaches for a used bar of Dial soap, handing it to me for the ailing man and strolls back to his office.

Seeking reinforcement, I call my best friend to tell her what happened and ask her what I should do. Through her laughter, I am realizing the hilarity of the situation. As we uncontrollably giggle, she receives a timely phone call from her husband who is out in Bristol Bay, commercial fishing. He erupts in laughter as she relays the scenario and then decides to share the story to a broader audience at sea.

I hang up with her and call our friend who is a nurse. Her husband answers, and says "she's not home." He is a doctor, so I shyly ask, "Do you mind if I ask you a question?" "Go ahead and I'll see if I know the answer," he responds. "Um. My husband... ah...er...well, he accidently sprayed his testicles with bear spray," I reluctantly share. "Well, I think I can offer some advice here," he leisurely explains. "The key ingredient in bear spray is capsaicin, a compound found in chili peppers." He goes on to tell me, "One evening I was chopping chili peppers for dinner with friends and then I went to use the bathroom. It was a painful experience. Anyway, the remedy is one-part bleach to ten parts water."

Cal is in a tub of water with the bleach faster than you can blink. He downs a few strong painkillers after his bath and arranges to take the next day off from work (an extremely rare occurrence).

That afternoon, I clean the gear out of the car from our adventure. With plastic gloves on my hands to protect my skin from the bear spray in his shorts and underwear, I chuckle a little as I hang the bright orange souvenirs up to dry.

A Trip Back East

Education is the key to unlocking the world,
a passport to freedom!

Oprah Winfrey

August of 2009, our 10th wedding anniversary, found me striving to produce positive results from my very difficult marriage. I spent some time considering renewing our vows with our extended families present, as our anniversary aligned with our annual trip to visit family on the east coast. At the time, I was still engaged in a serious effort to demonstrate my commitment to my husband and our family, with the hopes that he would join us, spiritually and emotionally.

Instead of renewing our vows, we had a very strained family trip that included an interview for my daughter with a private high school in Massachusetts, Phillips Academy Andover.

After years of my husband tearing down my efforts around the home, including my work to educate our daughter, I worked with Clara to ensure that she apply to a private high school. Cal interfered with her admissions essays and refused to talk about the tuition. Clara was under constant pressure. I knew once she got out the door, real life would start for her. My faith was still strong, but I did not understand God's plan. I just knew that our lives had become unbearable. I was going to do everything I could to help Clara salvage a piece of normal childhood.

The campus at Phillips Academy Andover was stunning and beautiful. The classrooms would have a small teacher to student ratio and Clara would have access to higher learning that would prepare her for anything she wanted to achieve in her life.

Our interviewer, Kevin, was exactly how I pictured he would be: outgoing, confident, and welcoming.

"Mr. and Mrs. Bering, we hope you enjoyed the tour of the campus!"

"Oh we did," I said. "It was excellent. Your student tour guide is so well spoken and knowledgeable. She did a very nice job answering our questions. She seems really involved in this school!"

"Thanks for saying so Mrs. Bering. If Clara is ready, we will interview her first and then we will come back for you and Mr. Bering."

"I think she's watching the video on student life here at Phillips. I'll just go get her."

After Clara's interview, we joined her in Kevin's office.

"Hi Clara," I said smiling at her as we entered the small office space.

"Welcome. Have a seat," Kevin said in a warm, friendly tone.

"Your daughter is a very articulate, well-spoken teenager. You must be very proud of her," said Kevin. "Let me tell you a little bit about the parent interview and why we value meeting with the whole family as you are considering our school.

"Phillips is a great school and offers an excellent education. However, it's important to us that we are a fit for you and that your student is a fit for our campus."

It was not long into the discussion that Cal began to sabotage the admissions interview by tensely asking the administrator endless highly combative questions.

"Kevin, Clara was brought up in a very conservative household. Are the boys allowed in the girls' dorms?"

"Yes, the boys are allowed in the girls' dorms."

"I see. Do you have a curfew for when the boys have to leave the girls dorms?"

"Cal I understand that your daughter would be living away from home for the first time and that this can be a difficult transition for parents. Clara would be matriculated into Phillips as a Junior."

Cal talked over him, "Is there supervision in the dorms during their free time? Like..."

"Cal, I'd like to ask Kevin a few questions," I interrupted as Cal's questioning increasingly went nowhere and the room was getting incredibly tense. Clara radiated anger, shifting in her seat.

"Kevin you mentioned that the students are highly focused on their own academic success and athletic success. I think Clara will really enjoy being amongst peers who she can learn from and grow with intellectually. Do the kids have study groups and ways to encourage each other's success? What do they do for fun? Do you find that there is a lot of school spirit with current students and alumni?"

"Definitely. There are many options for the kids to get involved and to really develop their interests. The student who brought you on a tour before this interview is the editor for the school newspaper. Just in the time I've spent interviewing Clara I have observed that she may really enjoy being a contributor to our school newspaper, among many other available options for her to get involved."

"Thank you so much for taking the time to meet with us. It was a pleasure speaking with you."

We all rose from our seats.

"You are welcome. It was very nice to meet you. I look

forward to Clara being a student here next fall!"

We left the interview and hopped into our rental car. I looked at Cal with frustration.

"Why were you harping on the curfew issue?"

"Yeah Dad. That was awful."

"These private schools are so full of money. They write books about kids partying and doing drugs at schools like this. Kevin was unprepared for the interview. I was asking appropriate questions regarding sending my daughter off to school. He should have been able to answer me more efficiently."

"Look, I got a good education at a public high school, and I got into Princeton. She can do just as well in a public school if not better. I don't want people thinking we are trying to keep up with the Joneses and acting all privileged."

"It was an interview. No decisions have been made..."

"Guys. Just stop."

Years later as a young adult, remembering our home-life with Cal, Clara offered that Cal used gas-lighting, financial abuse, and constant browbeating ranging from housework, my intelligence, my partnership with him, to spiritual abuse with a corrupt use of biblical principles. She said he treated me like not-human property. She stated, "It made us all sad, worried, and scared to witness."

The Evening of the Sisters

The trouble is that once you see it,
you can't unsee it.
And once you've seen it, keeping quiet,
saying nothing becomes as political
an act as speaking out.
There's no innocence either way,
you're accountable.

Arundhati Roy

Economic exploitation, isolation, and emotional manipulation are key forms of intimate partner abuse. These are all forms of power and control over another person that were masterfully put to use by Cal.

While still visiting in Massachusetts, we were invited to join my family and long-time friends for dinner at a local eatery. Cal and I headed off to the restaurant, but we never made it in to join them. Instead, we sat in the car pondering the truth of our marriage. The information that I needed to protect my children from this man was still not known to me.

"The only thing that will prevent the breakup of our marriage is a miracle," I said to him. "Are you willing to hold my hand and pray for a miracle?" He half-heartedly agreed with me. I lead the prayer, holding Cal's hand. "God, we need a miracle to repair this marriage. It is so broken, but we know you can repair anything. Please heal us. In Jesus name we pray."

As the twilight faded into shadowy darkness, the quiet engine of our black SUV rental car carried us to his mother's opulent home. Cal switched off the bright headlights shining on the cold wrought iron gate and my gaze fixed on the raven-black fence etched against the ominous starless night. Beyond the barrier, enticing long wispy beach grass rustled in the breeze, surrounding the illuminated saltwater pool. Joan's carefully crafted landscape oozed a façade of easy living.

Looking across to the driver's side of the vehicle I said, "Cal, maybe we should move closer to family. It might support the health of our marriage if we have our brothers' and sisters' families around and outside input into our lives."

The glow of the dashboard light dimly outlined Cal's face as he looked at me with bitter disgust.

"Josephine, if you can get a job that supports us at the level that I support us in Alaska, I will move back near family with you."

"I've been home raising children for more than a decade. I don't have enough work experience to support a family of five," I conceded.

The next evening Cal's stepfather, Dean, exclaimed "Can I say something? You want to know who is smart? It's *the Clara.* She's something!" In typical Gatsby fashion, he cheerfully announced, "How about we celebrate *the Clara!* Let's all go out to dinner tonight."

We arrived at the Port Island Grill at 7:00pm, finely dressed for an evening out. Cal's sister Shelley and his stepsisters, Terry and Mary, their significant others, his mother Joan, step-father Dean, Clara, Cal and I all surrounded a lovely candle-lit, linen covered table. The restaurant was once a clam shack that I enjoyed as a kid, but today fine wine and four star meals were served to our party of thirteen. Seizing an opportunity to be part of the celebration, I raised a glass to toast my tenth wedding anniversary with Cal. My husband had a look of childish surprise as he impishly held up his wine glass to my toast. Cal's family barely acknowledged me.

After dessert, I invited my in-laws to the beach house where Cal and I were staying with our children. Cal's brother Rusty and his father Cal, Sr. joined the gathering later in the evening.

Seated on the screened-in porch next to my sister-in-law, Shelley, I glanced at her father confidently leaning against the wall, absorbed in conversation. Grasping for some insight, I probed, "I am trying to figure out what is wrong with Cal. He is so emotionally removed. Is there any family history of Asperger's, or something? I mean is Cal a lot like your father? They just seem to have a really a similar demeanor."

She continued the conversation with a question I could never have anticipated.

"You know Cal molested me, right?"

I stammered at her shocking revelation. "Have you gotten counseling? Can I ask questions? I am sorry that this happened to you."

Shelley and I moved inside to the quiet of the dining room. She sat in the chair next to me. Her stepsisters Terry and Mary followed us and sat across the table.

"Who knows about this?" I asked.

"I've known," Terry answered. Mary remained quiet.

"He apologized to me, so I thought you knew. I never would have said anything but I wanted you to know for Clara's safety," said Shelley.

Clara's safety? She is already fourteen years old, I thought to myself. Then I asked, "What did he do? Did you tell your parents?"

Shelly answered, "I would wake up out of my sleep and find him in my room touching me or masturbating. I told my father, but he said he didn't hear me. I asked my parents to put a lock on my door and that is when he stopped molesting me."

In shock, I defensively claimed, "Well, he's never done anything like that to my family. Can I ask more questions if I need to know more information?"

Cal walked into the room and said, "What's going on in here? Looks so serious."

"Hey Cal. I was just leaving" said Terry.

"Yeah. It's been a long night. I'm tired. See you later Cal, Josephine."

"Good night, Mary."

"Well, I'm going to head out too. Good night!"

"Good night Shelley."

The conversation was quietly overheard by fourteen-year-old Clara as she pretended to have her face in a book on a nearby couch. This evening became known between Clara and I as the "Evening of the Sisters." Temporarily, the sisters let their wall down. In this pivotal moment, they were revealing imperative information to me—too late.

The next day, I phoned his mother and asked her if she knew of the abuse that had gone on in her home.

"Yes, I knew. But I didn't think I should disrupt an entire family for the actions of a 14-year-old boy."

"What am I supposed to do with this information?" I asked her. "What do I say to him?"

"Well, I think you should go to him and ask him why he did not tell you."

* * *

70

As we prepared to leave our beach house in Massachusetts for a long drive to my sister Alice's lake house in Maine, silence filled my mouth. My brain couldn't form words. My heart was trying to enclose the depravity of my husband's actions towards his sister, to keep this degradation away from all others. My body manifested the destruction he had caused, as tears pouring out of my eyes. We arrived at the lake house as the family reunion weekend was already underway.

"Clara, please help Jason out of his car seat for me," I whispered, as Cal took a parking spot in the cramped driveway. Without hesitation, Clara scooped her youngest brother up onto her skinny, teenage hip and grabbed Andrew's hand. Through a mental fog, I watched as my three children escaped with my nieces and nephews, running down the steep, treelined path toward the lakefront where their grandfather stood in his bright-yellow sunshirt, welcoming them.

Walking through the grassy side yard, I greeted my brother-in-law, Richard, with a quick hug as he prepped the grill to feed the army of family members. I added my bundle of groceries to the red and white picnic table overflowing with bags of chips, brownies, and half-drunk soda cans abandoned by over-excited children.

Looking for my sisters, I passed by coolers filled with beverages as I opened the creaky backdoor, stepped up on the old cement landing, and found myself standing in the kitchen.

"Josephine, you're here!" Adele's smile changed as she read my face.

Alice warmly hugged me and gently stepped back with her hand on my shoulder. "Josephine, what's wrong?"

Gazing at the wood floor, I motioned my head to say "no", because words were not available. My siblings were helpless, unable to comfort me as they looked upon my speechless, dazed presence.

* * *

That night, after all the cousins, aunts, uncles, grand-parents, and our children had gone to bed, I approached Cal.

"Can I speak to you a moment?"

He indifferently followed me to the porch where we sat on the worn couch together. The lake was barely visible, obscured by the shadows of the tall trees dominating our surroundings.

"Shelley told me that you molested her," I stated softly.

His face suddenly turned white, dusty looking. His eyes hollowed out in fear. Several minutes passed, then he responded, "Yes I molested Shelley. I molested my youngest stepsister, Mary, too. When I was a kid."

She's younger than you by eleven years.

"You were 13 or 14 years old. Did you take off her diaper?"

"Yes. It was like a science experiment."

"Were you aroused?"

"Yes."

After very careful consideration, I quietly asked, "Have you ever touched Clara?"

As I watched him pause to craft his response, sparks of fear went shrieking through my blue veins.

"I don't know," he whispered. "I might have held her in a funny way. When I was carrying her to bed, I might have had my hand on her breast."

Shelley's words echoed through me: *I would wake up out of my sleep and find him in my room touching me.*

"And there was a time...when we were on our way to Hawaii," Cal continued. "We were in our hotel room, and we were all asleep in the same bed. That time, I...I was confused when we were all sleeping in the same bed and I might have thought Clara was you."

Wait. What? How old was Clara, ten?

This was the first time I had ever seen vulnerability in him. But this did not look like the vulnerability of a remorseful man; rather it was the look of a man terrified of being caught.

Early the next morning I walked upstairs to the room that my parents were sharing.

"Mom, Dad, I know you have seen me upset. I'm struggling to find words to tell you... Cal's sister, Shelley, told me that Cal molested her when they were kids. I quietly confronted him last night. He volunteered that he had also molested his younger stepsister, Mary."

Later that morning, as my mother and I walked through the sunny lakeside neighborhood, leading us to the privacy of a peaceful old New England graveyard, she stopped and pointed to a gravestone.

"Life is short," she said. "Forgive him and move on."

Shortly thereafter, we returned home to Alaska. The torment of what I had learned was gripping my chest like an exhale that could not escape. I needed acknowledgment that I wasn't overreacting and that this was real. In a weekly session with our family counselor, Erin, I shared all that I had found out back east. Her response stunned me.

"You know I have to notify the Office of Children's Services?" My heart dropped as I realized the privacy and the dignity of my family was slipping away.

"Cal, our therapist is reporting your abuse of Shelley and Mary to OCS."

"What?! You didn't fucking check before doing that?!"

"Check what?" I fearfully asked him.

His shoulders were pinned up around his ears as he scowled at me. "Like fucking check with your parents for legal advice to find out if it was safe to tell our counselor that I abused my sisters!"

"Cal, I had no idea that the counselor was going to report abuse that happened twenty years ago in another state. Therefore, I did not think to ask my parents about their legal opinion on the matter."

That night Clara was working on her school project.

"Dad, where is the computer?"

Cal simply replied, "It wasn't working properly. I threw it out."

"But I have important stuff for school projects and photos saved on the computer!" She pleaded.

"Cal, you threw out an entire computer? Are you serious? Don't you have to take that to the hazardous waste or something? You just dumped it?" I inquired. He just walked away from me. *Why would he throw out the computer?*

His heightened, erratic behavior over the next few days was exposing a side of him that I had never seen. One day Andrew came to me as I was folding laundry in my bedroom,

"Mom! Dad's smashing the glass toilet in the backyard!"

Toilet? From the bathroom remodel? I watched through the bedroom window as he was recklessly smashing the porcelain toilet with a maul. The destructiveness of his instability was threatening. He was losing control over his emotions, and our family. His cover was unraveling and my instincts were becoming more clear. *There is something really, really wrong with this man.* When I later attempted to document the destruction with a photo, Cal had already, uncharacteristically, cleared all the porcelain debris away.

In the following days we tolerated our normal routines,

maintaining a perceived normalcy. We were working together to stack the cord of wood that had been delivered as the phone rang.

"Hello?"

"Josephine." Joan's voice trembled.

Hearing tears in her voice for the first time ever, I thought she was calling to console me about Cal's actions and our deteriorating marriage.

"Dean died."

Dean had been nervous about his heart valve replacement surgery that he would undergo days after we left the east coast. He had even jokingly quipped, "I am going to take a dirt nap."

"Oh Joan, I am so sorry." I was in disbelief. Dean was such a life force.

"I am just afraid the girls are going to think I did it."

"Oh Joan, of course they are not going to think that. Let me get Cal for you."

Cal hung up the phone with slumped shoulders and said, "I just feel bad because I didn't even like him." Cal made immediate arrangements to return to the east coast for the imminent funeral.

After the reality of losing Dean had settled in a little, we resumed family counseling sessions with Erin to begin to address what I thought were the extent of Cal's, and therefore our, issues. Erin recommended Cal consult with his own therapist. He hired Dr. Daniel Kessler, a psychologist with a Ph.D., whom he sought out to document his willingness to "confront his issues and learn about his blind spots."

After Cal and I started meeting separately with Dr. Kessler, Erin approached me privately with the idea of open communication between the counselors.

"Josephine, if Cal is serious about getting help, let's have you both sign a release of information so we can work together with his therapist. This way he will be held more accountable. He needs to focus on his underlying issues so my counseling will be more effective." She compassionately added, "He will need time to process his counseling sessions because they will be intense for him."

I looked at her, unconvinced. Nervously, I pinned my palms facing each-other between my knees as my face flushed with dread. "That may work. However, I'm still concerned as to how Dr. Kessler was able to disregard me when I told him that Cal masturbated in Clara's room. He told me that was 'pushing the envelope, but it wasn't abuse.' He also told me that it's normal that Cal won't let me purchase silverware or curtains."

I had been researching the symptoms in my relationship and even brought books to share with Dr. Kessler that I found, *Walking on Eggshells* and *Inside the Minds of Angry and Abusive Men*. He didn't consider or acknowledge my attempts to find answers.

I felt like I was pleading with my own therapist to be heard.

"How am I supposed to believe that this open counseling will help?"

Family Man

You think our lives are cheap
And easy to be wasted
As history repeats
So foul you can taste it

Lauryn Hill
I Find It Hard To Say (Rebel)

Through therapy, in the fall of 2009, Cal appeared to be seeking ways to become a more supportive family man. At the same time, I was searching for ways to become stronger and healthier. I believed that, since Cal had been confronted with his past, he could be honest with himself and bless others. Soon I would discover that he had not disclosed all of his victims.

His family didn't give me the consideration of telling me what they knew. They were willing to sacrifice Clara's innocence for their image. Carefully withholding information so as to deprive me of my right to make an informed decision about my life's partner and the safety of my children.

Cal created then exploited my struggle. By late September he was playing hero and introduced the idea of hiring a part-time nanny. He arranged an interview with Carette, a 28-year-old woman that he purportedly found on Craigslist, to "help" with Jason and Andrew. She provided us with references that Cal claimed he verified and then he hired her.

Accepting my husband's efforts and trusting that he had chosen a capable person who would keep his children safe, allowed me to follow the therapist's advice and take some time to focus on myself. I decided to get back into racing shape, train for a marathon, take a doula course to increase my knowledge for teaching my prenatal yoga class, and I began to get more serious about my own yoga practice.

Training for my first marathon brought me camaraderie and gave me a chance to breathe. My friend Annie and I accomplished our goal, both completing our first marathon in Jacksonville, Florida in late February, 2010. As I had been preparing to travel to Florida, Cal convinced me to extend my trip and visit my good friends who were living and working in Nicaragua. Reluctantly, I accepted his strange plan that separated me from my young family for 10 days. Carette stayed with our family to help with the children while I was away.

Distance from Cal proved to offer me mental clarity, but phone calls with my children drew me back to their reality. It sounded like they needed me to be home. Clara was overburdened. Andrew missed me. Jason wasn't interested in being on the phone. Upon my arrival home, I found an entitled man and three distant children. They were too young for me to be gone for so long and in hindsight they were never safe in Cal's presence.

Jason clung to me each time Carette's car pulled up in the driveway. He hid behind me and stuck his tongue out at her. He said to Carette, "I hate you." I was trying to teach him to be nice to her and I was very surprised by his behavior. I was doing chores and work around the house and I noticed Carette hovered over Jason at the kitchen table, forcing her body on him and ignoring his personal space. Noticing his discomfort, spontaneously, I commented, "I don't force my children to hug people." Jason pushed her away, demonstrating his autonomy.

Her undersized yellow teeth clenched, forming a grin that was intended to look friendly.

In a syrupy voice she said, "Be nice Jason."

I stopped what I was doing, stepped in front of her, looking into her small green eyes, I instructed her, "Carette. Please give him some space." Like a smoker's cough, Carette's flirty giggle jostled in her windpipe as she busied herself with some of Jason's art supplies.

Soon after, Carette disappeared, retreating to Hawaii. Over a month went by and she contacted Cal upon her return to Alaska. A few days a week she commenced caring for Jason, and sometimes Andrew. Jason would cling to me for dear life when Carette showed up and say really mean things to her. Cal didn't report noticing anything strange about Carette's treatment of Jason. One day as she was leaving my house, her face grew ashen as she fell into a panic looking for her camera. Together, we searched all over my house for the missing camera and she expressed an immense gasp of relief, quickly clutching the apparatus from my hand after I discovered it in the guest bedroom.

Jason had just turned four years old in March, and I was hosting my bible study group friends at my weekly *Waffles and Coffee Tuesday*. After delighting in waffles, coffee and warm conversation, we all hiked the trail behind my house. Walking with my friends Katie and Brynn, I gestured my eyes towards the running stroller I was pushing. Jason was slumped over in the stroller, limp, while the other small children were running and jumping through the mud puddles. I said, "Guys, I don't know what I'm seeing. He said he doesn't want to be alive and that his favorite color is no longer purple, it's black."

"Josephine," Brynn offered, "there's an article in *The New York Times Magazine* about childhood depression. Maybe it has some helpful information?"

In April of 2010 I arranged for a week-long escape to New York City to study with one of my prenatal yoga mentors. Carette stayed at my house and took care of my children in my absence. When I got home, Jason was rigid and distant. *Was this his way of communicating that he missed me?* Later that evening, at his bath time, I found a bruised abrasion on his sternum. He was defensive about his bruise and wouldn't give me any information. Carette was unreachable. Cal had no explanation.

"Nothing was out of the ordinary, Josephine. You need to stop being so hypersensitive."

A month and a half went by, and I craved the newfound freedom and independence that traveling alone and meeting new people provided for me. I planned one final, solo trip to New Mexico, to camp up in the mountains during summer solstice and experience a whole new culture, while increasing my knowledge on the healing aspects of yoga and Ayurvedic medicine. Cal staged an incredible resistance to this trip. He didn't want me to go, either because he didn't want to spend his *and my* money on my trip, or he feared I was slipping from his grasp. In the midst of conversation, while I was arranging my travel, he casually commented: "I'm afraid something might've happened to Jason the last time you were away." *What is he talking about?*

We argued: "Cal are you suggesting that Jason is not safe when I leave?"

"No. Josephine, I just think he is impacted by your absence."

"I'm sure he is, but you continuously tell me that there is no problem when I'm not around and that I create all the tension in the household."

Not knowing what to believe, and desperately seeking the mental clarity that presented itself whenever I was not in Cal's company, I followed through with my plans, even under his immense pressure to stay. In my heart, anything I could do to become stronger and hold our marriage together was what I would do. Strengthening my vision for our family's future required that I develop autonomy and could be less of a burden on the family *as Cal constantly said that I was a burden.*

Shortly after my trip to New Mexico we left for our annual family vacation to Massachusetts. Against my better judgment, Carette would house sit for us while we were away. During this trip Jason's quiet, rigid demeanor morphed into unremitting aggressive behavior that could not be soothed. This was a sharp contrast to the playful, sweet little boy I knew. Something was very wrong. My questions hung in the air with no response.

"Clara, did you notice anything odd with Carette's care of Jason? Did you see them together? Andrew, what was she like when you got home from school? Cal, what do you think is going on with Jason?"

After a stressful family trip witnessing Jason's wildly unsettled behavior, we returned to a vacant, eerily unkempt home. I began unpacking the boys clothing from their luggage and discovered dried vomit on the dresser, in the drawers, and on the toy shelves.

"Cal, the neighbor said that the driveway was filled with cars on several occasions while we were away. Carette must have had a party here. The place is not clean. I just found dried puke in the boys' bedroom. This was not what we had agreed upon. Do not pay her."

Carette blithely pulled into the driveway wearing her yellow grin and seeking payment. I walked her into the house and confronted her, pointing out the dried vomit and the messy house. Her face washed over with an element of fear, and a strong desire to avoid confrontation. She claimed that the crusty brown vomit splattered all over the bedroom was dried paint.

"Are you telling me this is paint?" I asked, holding up the bright orange paint bottle next to the dried vomit. I said, "Carette, you are lying to my face."

Her willingness to lie accompanied by her insensitive request for money left me discovering a whole new breed of human. She retreated like a cockroach in the light, out the front door and into the driveway where she met with Cal. I watched in astonishment as Cal opened his wallet and paid her a large sum of money. That was the last time we had Carette in our home. Never again would I trust Cal to find care for our children.

Although I could not yet verbalize the new understanding that was occurring for me, I was, for the first time, experiencing a budding awareness that Cal was operating on a different frequency. My need for help with the children was still relevant because of their ages and now because Jason was broken. Reaching out to close friends for childcare resources, I was introduced to and immediately impressed with Hannah. The contrast in Jason's reception of her illuminated the alarming care that Carette had provided for him. It was immediately obvious that Jason absolutely loved Hannah, through his words and his body language.

"I hate that you let Carette babysit us," he said. "Hannah only."

Cal receded to the background as I investigated Jason's suffering and overt personality change. Seeking answers and support, I relied on my best friends from my Bible study group, who rallied around Jason and me. One evening I invited them to my house specifically to pray for Jason and lighten the atmosphere of the home. He knew Kayla, Stella, and Janie very well. His rigid anger was replaced with a soft gaze and trust. When they arrived, I saw the little boy I hadn't seen in months as he curled up in Kayla's lap like a baby. His eyes relaxed as Janie, who was wearing an oversized white sweatshirt that covered her pregnant belly, gently put her hand on his shoulder. Stella spoke lovingly to Jason, her voice very familiar and warm. Jason was calm and secure.

Even in the company of what truly felt like angels, his momentary relief did not last. Jason didn't have the power to control what was raging inside of him, or more likely, the safety of trusted adults allowed him to act out his experience and show us what had happened to him. He began to thrash violently and thrust himself out of Kayla's arms. She remained seated on the sage green rug, where she had been gently holding him. He angled towards the window and vaulted off the bed, in what appeared to be an attempt to jump out the window. Stella and Janie blocked him, held him momentarily, but he kept lunging toward the window. Kayla then stood in his sight and he began to sob. He crawled back in her arms and fell asleep. She tucked him in his warm bed, where he slept soundly until the next morning. While he slept, we said prayers for his healing. The next morning he woke me up and said, "I didn't dream last night. No nightmares."

His personality change persisted though, and in the wake of severing ties with Carette, Jason's expressions grew progressively more disturbing. By fall, his rage was mixed with sexualized behaviors. His therapist told me that the acting out was latent because it takes time for children to process their trauma. The acting out was positive for his recovery because it meant that he was not internalizing the abuse.

On one occasion, based on his acting out, I said to him "No adult is allowed to touch you anywhere on your body that is not covered by a bathing suit."

He replied, "You have to tell *them* that!" Who did he mean by *them*? And what had *they* been doing with him? He was flicking and hitting and yelling "go to your room!!!" repetitively. Or "shut up!!" He covered his ears with his hands and sang, "Ear muffs. I can't heaaarrr you." Also, parroting words that had been said to him, he blurted out "Your mother is in a far-off land and can't help you." He said that the scariest place, the worst place where she would hurt him was in her car.

From September 2010 through March of 2011 I made notes and voice recordings of Jason's alarming comments and actions. I wanted to be able to document the moment Jason said the name, or names of who had hurt him.

Abbreviated excerpt of the least distressing notes:

September 17, 2010

Jason woke up 5:15am from a bad dream. Someone cut his head off and drown him under water.

September 18, 2010

Jason was stressed out and I asked him what happened.

"I hate your mother," he said with a far-off look in his eyes.

<u>September 20, 2010</u>

Jason wet his bed last p.m.
Jason yells out with anger in his face, "Carette spanks me! All the time!"
"Carette talks mean to me."
"Carette punched me like 50 times in the stomach with my clothes on."

<u>September 28, 2010</u>

- Jason said "If I do this for you, you have to listen to me forever. Listen to me! I'll do you a favor. Listen to meeee!"
- "Oh well, sorry. My ears are plugged. I can't hear you." Jason says to me. Then he says "I hate that you let Carette babysit us."
- "Wee fishy shop. Carette got the dog a bone there."
- We read a book about feelings and he liked the happy picture but said he never feels happy. He says he's never happy.
- He said he had none of the feelings in the book.
- Jason had a very hard time listening to a book about love. He now has no tolerance for affection.
- He said "fuck" at dinner time.
- We asked him not to and he said he didn't have to listen.

- Earlier today I talked to Jason about how other people aren't allowed to touch us and he said "I'll kill them."

- Carry you to a car and bring you to another place. Kill the police."

- He hopes "they kill the babysitter."

October 23, 2010

1. Can he be healed of this stuff?

2. When is a brain scan ordered?

3. How do I stop worrying about not being there to protect him and how he suffered?

4. How do I get over my bad choice and lack of discernment in allowing Carette to babysit and Cal to find her on Craigslist?

5. How do I heal from this betrayal?

6. How do I prevent this type of person entering in my life and our lives?

7. Can I trust in the justice system, that it will serve my son?

8. How can I assure that he will be best served by the justice system?

9. Do predators have free reign b/c kids can't identify the experience w enough clarity?

10. How do I deal w my anger at the woman who hurt him?

October 30, 2010

Notes from interactions with Jason:

1. Jason's stuffed animal "puppy" has parents who died. Last night he told me that puppy's parents were "shot and killed and that the bad guy didn't get puppy b/c he hid behind a tree."

2. Jason said puppy wanted to sleep with me "but not dad." He said "puppy didn't like the dad and puppy wants to sleep with mom and Jason."

November 24, 2010

Comments from Jason:
"Do this or I'll kill your dog."
"I have to wait for the camera to load." (We don't have a camera that loads)
Jason started refusing to be in any photos

January 4, 2011

Notes to Sophia - Jason's therapist.
Jason and I were telling stories. He began a story about fairies who had mean babysitters. In the story two fairies were sharing their bad babysitter experiences. One fairy had a boy sitter the other had a girl sitter. He added to the story that when the sitter was mean "you wished you could make yourself smaller than a speck so they couldn't find you."

January 16, 2011

1) Evil exists.

2) She hurt my son.
3) Pretended to be my friend
4) He is a different kid.
5) I can barely remember the Jason before her abuse.

<u>*February 10, 2011*</u>

To Sophia:
Today was a hard day for Jason. He hit, pinched and laughed at his little friends. And it also becomes a day of Jason the troublemaker when he's always behaving poorly. I could use a lot of help with this.
My friends' children are going to lose patience and trust in Jason, quickly. It's going to further his beliefs that he is shamed.

In the deepest core of my soul I knew Carette was responsible for the drastic change in Jason's behavior and spirit. What friends close to me suspected at the time, that I couldn't yet acknowledge, was that there may have been a connection between Carette and Cal. Over time my suspicions grew that Cal had known Carette in some capacity before hiring her. Later, during the criminal trial, Cal included Carette among the people on his witness list that he was going to have testify against Clara.

FBI

He's not dead. Just hijacked.

Sophia
Therapist for Jason

Walking down Loop Road in my red rain jacket, the air was filled with a mist from the glacier and the scent of cold wooded rain. It was September of 2010. I'd just dropped my 4-year-old son off at his nursery school. Walking out of the nursery school doors, the ache of my child's suffering coursed through my rib cage.

I dialed my father's phone.

"Dad, can you talk?"

"Josephine, your mother and I are at my reunion with the FBI in Quantico. Hold on a minute." His phone jostled and I heard rustling as he stepped away from the table into a more private setting. "What is going on?"

"Jason's telling me things; he's saying that his nanny 'punched him in the stomach like 50 times, *with his clothes on*.'"

"Josephine. Calm down. When did this happen? What is he saying? Where is he now?"

"He's in nursery school right now. I don't know exactly when this happened. Cal found this woman, Carette, by putting an advertisement on Craigslist last fall for a nanny. Andrew was in school or activities most of the time, so Jason

89

was alone with her frequently. He's telling me that she 'screamed at him all the time, in the house.' That she hit him. Dad, he acted out behaviors that were age-inappropriate. When I kindly said not to do that, he said, 'You have to tell *them* that.'"

"Where is the nanny?"

"She spends half her time in Hawaii and then she comes back to Alaska. She's from here, but I don't have an address."

"You don't have an address?! She crossed state lines. Have you called the police?"

"Yes. First I took him to see his pediatrician. He referred me to a social worker. She met with Jason and me. During the meeting he drew a picture of a large phallus and next to that a butterfly. He said the butterfly was his sister and she saved him. The therapist advised me to call the police. I also called the Office of Children's Services. He's had two forensic interviews with the Child Advocacy Center."

"Josephine. Holy shit. How are they handling this?"

"Dad, the police said he has clearly been traumatized but he will not speak to them. And I'm pretty sure they interviewed her too. I don't know what to do. I can't believe this is happening Dad."

"Josephine, take a breath. Hang up with me now and call the Federal Bureau of Investigation in Alaska. Tell the FBI that she crossed state lines."

"Ok."

Trembling with fear and anger, I walked in the misty rain near Deer Lake trail, heading towards the Glacier. Clearing the moisture off my cell phone, I pressed the numbers on the phone quickly before the rain made the screen too wet again. An agent answered the phone.

"My father is a former FBI agent, and he told me to call your office because our nanny abused my son."

"Ma'am, what is your name?"

"My name is Josephine Bering. In September of 2009, my husband placed an ad on Craigslist for a nanny for a three-year-old boy. Carette Ruse responded to his ad and we hired her to take care of Jason for the school year. She left Alaska and went to Hawaii. I don't have an address for her, only a phone number. My son is four years old now; he turned four in March."

"Do you have an address of where she was staying in Alaska?"

"No, but I have a phone number."

"You don't have an address for your nanny?"

"No, sir."

"Ma'am. I'm really sorry for what you are going through. Kids are resilient. Your son is going to be okay. I'm not really sure there is anything that I can do for you. All you have for me to go on is a phone number."

In quiet desperation, I thanked the agent and hung up the phone. I felt sick. I had assumed Cal was acting responsibly, hiring from Craigslist instead of the normal way that I usually arranged childcare, through friends. I felt so ashamed that I didn't do more to protect Jason.

I walked back toward the school, climbed into my blue Subaru Forester with an empty car seat in the back, and called my dad back.

"Hello," he said.

"Dad, the agent didn't feel like he could do anything for me."

"I'm so far away Josephine. I'm going to send you an email. Walk into the FBI office. Hand them this email."

I drove a mile to my house, printed up my dad's email, and then drove 12 miles to downtown and parked outside the Federal Building. Usually I was in this building to go to the Post

Office. Today, I went through the other line, towards the FBI agents.

Once through security, I walked through sterile glass doors to a bank of elevators. I stepped off the elevator and walked down an endless narrow corridor with shiny, spotless tiled flooring, and then down another long, narrow corridor. At the end, there was a door to my right. I knocked lightly on the door.

An agent about my height partially opened the door. My hand clasped the white piece of paper folded in half, containing my father's email message, and I squeezed my arm through the crack in the door to give this man the paper and to get him to acknowledge me. He read the paper and let me in the first room, which was the size of a closet.

"What do you want!? What do you want me to do!?" he said.

"I want you to listen to me!"

Our voices escalated quickly.

"My son was abused by his nanny! She crossed state lines. My dad is a former FBI agent and he said to come see you!"

He said, "Come in here."

We walked through another set of doors and sat at a small table. He listened to me as I recounted things my young son had said to me about being hit repeatedly, the nightmares, bedwetting, and the total change in personality. Based on the vocabulary he was using, it was clear to me that he had been exposed to some form of sexual activity. All I could think was that if I alerted enough people in the right places, my son would be healed. Maybe they had some technology that could identify my son's image, if he was used for child pornography. Somehow, I believed that if I knew what happened, I could undo the damage. It would take me almost a decade to learn that this was faulty thinking.

The agent's name was Steven. He said to me, "Your son is

going to be ok, ma'am."

After the intense meeting, without having time to process the conversation, I drove back to the nursery school to pick up my little boy.

Diagnoses

If you bungle raising your children,
I don't think whatever else you do matters very much.

Jacqueline Kennedy Onassis

God what am I supposed to do? My beautiful little boy is
shattered. Please heal my son. Please take this from him. Don't
let his life be destroyed.

The days were long as I, with an eviscerated heart, dug for
ways to find help for Jason. My mission was two-fold: I wanted
my son back and I wanted Carette taken out of circulation so
that children would be safe.

Prior to my meeting with the FBI agent, the aggregate of
Jason's mysterious injuries, change in personality, aggressive
behaviors and my concerns about childhood depression were
weighing on me and I brought him to a very experienced
pediatrician. After observing Jason's behaviors, the
pediatrician recommended that I contact a social worker. We
met with the social worker and she implored me to make a
report with the Office of Children's Services (OCS) about my
concerns. OCS arranged for the Child Advocacy Center (CAC)
to begin an investigation.

A second interview for Jason with the CAC was scheduled
after the first interview failed to yield any information. The law

enforcement officer came out of the interviewing room and said that Jason wouldn't reveal anything. Except, in a very pointed gesture, the officer looked right at Cal and said, "But he really doesn't like you."

Cal emotionlessly responded, "I know. That concerns me."

The social worker we were working with said that Alaska didn't have the forensic specialists that we needed. Researching resources all over the country, I discovered Bessel van der Kolk, a leading expert in trauma treatment at the Justice Resource Institute in the Boston area. I consulted with the social worker on my research, looking for guidance. She said, "Why don't you call the place in Boston? That way you will be near family and have support."

After my first phone call to initiate an evaluation for Jason, I spent a week in exhausting phone and email conversations to complete the intake process. I shared details about Jason's increasingly abnormal behaviors during and following Carette's 'care', and the extensive list of his comments and behaviors that I had documented. Jason was scheduled for a formal trauma evaluation at the Trauma Center, Justice Resource Institute in Brookline, Massachusetts. Simultaneously, Andrew was scheduled to be evaluated in nearby Connecticut.

Andrew and Jason's symptoms vastly differed. From what I had researched, Andrew's symptoms lined up with Asperger's syndrome. Each school year, I approached the teachers with the same concerns and requested services through the speech therapists. Finally, the school was willing to administer testing for my third grader that showed he would need occupational and speech therapy, but he was given low priority. "When we start to see a significant decline in his reading and writing, then he will be moved up in line for services."

I persisted in acquiring intervention for him, and with the

assistance of our pediatrician, Andrew finally received the care I was seeking for him in the Developmental Disabilities Clinic at the Yale Child Study Center. Andrew's evaluations coincided with Jason's forensic interview, during our emergency trip to the east coast for Jason. Years of searching for ways to uncover and address Andrew's needs and help him to grow into a productive member of society had finally come around to this clinic, where I hoped to get the guidance I needed to help him.

Clara couldn't miss school, so we arranged for her to stay with friends while Cal and I traveled together to Boston with her brothers. Medical appointments were confirmed, schools were notified that the boys would be absent, and airfare was arranged. I believed that expert care was going to provide relief.

The day before our trip, Cal and I hiked a nearby mountain and shared our expectations for the boys. Cal surprised me when he opposed the plans set in motion to have Andrew evaluated. "I don't think Andrew needs this testing. It's a waste. What if he is taking the place of a kid who really needs this testing, and it turns out that nothing is wrong? How're you going to feel then?"

Deeply grieved by his resistance, I once again found myself trying to convince my husband of the obvious.

"We are responsible for this child. If it turns out that he is fine, then we will know that we did all that we could to ensure that his needs were met."

Cal continued his objection to the care I was seeking for the boys, even after we had arrived at our hotel in Connecticut.

"Andrew! Go stand in the hallway."

"Dad, what did I do?"

"You won't stop fooling around with your brother and I'm trying to get my work done!"

"Dad, I'll stop. I didn't know I was doing anything wrong.

Jason won't stop hitting me and flicking me. Please don't make me stand in the hallway."

Cal opened the hotel door and forced Andrew into the hallway.

"No thank you. I'm fine." I heard Andrew's voice say to a stranger. "My Dad asked me to stand out here because my little brother and me were aggravating him while he was trying to get work done."

I opened the door and pulled Andrew back into the hotel room.

Andrew's cognitive testing lasted three days at the Yale Child Study Center. On the last day of the process, I sat alone with the specialists while Cal traveled north to Boston with Jason. Upon the completion of the clinical evaluations, it was finally determined that Andrew was not on the Autism spectrum.

"So what are we looking at?" I asked.

"Anxiety," I was informed. Nine-year-old Andrew was plagued by anxiety so severe that it was impairing his executive functioning.

The team of professionals affirmed that I had done the right thing by bringing him in for testing. He was found to have a unique learning style and he would likely benefit from speech and occupational therapy. Years of my concerns over Andrew's developmental warning signs had been honored, valued, and discussed. The words of the top speech therapist in the team of evaluators were like grout in tiling—connecting the pieces and making sense of my emotions: "You did the right thing by bringing your child here to be evaluated. Don't second guess yourself."

* * *

While I was finishing meeting with the Yale specialists, Cal brought Jason to the first of five forensic interview sessions that would take place over the following two weeks. He convinced me that it would be better for Jason if he was not clinging to me before he arrived at the Trauma Center.

A few days later, we both brought Jason to his second appointment. Cal and Jason sat in the waiting room while I let the receptionist know we had arrived.

"Oh, you are here early! Yesterday, Jason and his father took the wrong train and they were quite late for Jason's first day of testing."

Cal doesn't get lost and he doesn't waste time or money, I thought to myself.

"That's strange." I said to the receptionist. "My husband used to work in Boston and he's meticulous with planning ahead. I'm really sorry that they were late."

"Oh, it was fine. Cal and Jason arrived in good spirits; laughing and giggling."

Cal does not giggle. And Jason does not show any interest in Cal. I filed the receptionist's feedback in my head because her description of Cal and Jason's arrival was very uncharacteristic of each of them.

Cal left for Alaska the day before our final meetings were scheduled with the specialists so he could go on a hunting trip with his friends, leaving me to fly across the country with our two young boys. Anyone remotely near us in the airport observed that 4-year-old Jason was totally out of his mind. His abnormal behaviors were pronounced. I could not take my attention off him for one second. This left nine-year-old Andrew to fend for himself. On the plane, Jason screamed and was tossing himself around, hitting, swearing, tearing at things, and pulling on people. Emotionally and physically depleted, I began to come to terms with the fact that all of us were manifesting years of living under *immense pressure*.

After waiting patiently for Jason's trauma evaluation, it arrived: twenty-seven pages long, recounting a summary of changes in behavior, events that led to our decision to seek help, notations of recent caregivers, our family history, Jason's developmental, social and medical history, and prior treatment. Each of the five private interviews with my son were recorded in great detail.

Trauma Center at JRI, excerpt from the fifth session:

The evaluator said that the last time they met, they had talked about babysitters, and he had said he hates Carette the most. She told him she was interested in hearing what makes him hate her the most. Jason did not make eye contact and did not respond. The evaluator wondered if it was something Carette said, or something she did. Jason said, "I don't want to talk about this." He had been playing with a pad of post-it notes, drawing on them. He took one of post-its and placed it on top of the evaluator's pad of paper. She asked if he could tell her why he doesn't want to talk about it? He said he didn't know.

Asked what kinds of things he and Carette did together, he did not respond. Asked if they did errands together, if they went in the car, Jason said, "Andrew went in the car with her too." Asked where they would go, he said he did not know. Asked if she took him places, he did not respond. Asked if she brought people to the house, he said,

"Three times. I don't want to talk about this."
Asked if she brought grown-ups to the house, he
said, "No." Asked if she brought kids to the house,
he said, "No."

Jason started drawing large letter "X"s on post-its,
and putting them over the evaluator's writing on
her pad of paper. He said, "Covering up words so
you're gonna have some trouble." The evaluator
noted that he was covering up the words she was
writing.

The evaluator said to him that he told his Mom
some things about Carette, that Carette punched
you in the stomach. He said, "Oh no, she didn't."
Asked if he remembers telling his Mom that
Carette punched him he did not respond. Asked if
he remembers telling his Mom that Carette
spanked him, he did not immediately respond,
then said, "I don't want to talk about it." He drew
an X on a post-it and placed in on the pad of paper.
"Because I don't want to be talking about this." He
continued placing post-its over the entire page.

The evaluator asked if he thought he could talk to
his Mom about it. He said, "Yes." The evaluator
asked what feeling he has when he thinks about
Carette. He said he didn't know. Asked if the
feeling is happy, sad, mad, worried, or scared, he
said, "Mad." The evaluator clarified that when he
thinks about Carette he feels mad. Jason said,
"Yeah. But I'm putting an X here. You already
asked that." He drew an X on another post-it and
placed it on the paper.

The evaluator wrote on a page underneath the page with the post-its. He continued to place post-its on the top page during the next conversation. The evaluator stated that his Mom says that he is using words that people in his family don't like. Jason did not immediately respond, then said that "Clara says shit and she says dang it and shut up too. And she says mean words but not to her friends." Asked if Andrew says words that they are not supposed to use, he said he does not. Jason put more post-its on the paper and said, "Finally, all these words are covered up." The evaluator said that it is important for their Mom and Dad to know about things that happen to the kids, so that they can help. She noted that she tells kids who come to this office that they won't get in trouble for talking about things.

The evaluator acknowledged that he doesn't want to answer these questions today. He said, "No, I'm getting sleepy." She asked who he would talk to, his Mom? Jason did not respond. Asked if he would talk to his Dad, Jason said, "I just X-ed out so I don't have to answer. I'm just gonna X 'em out and X 'em out and X 'em out."

Just as he had been with me, Jason did not, or was not able to report his experience. The experts had not been able to help. As a mother, it felt like a failed attempt to once again protect my child. However, there was validation in the report, noted by perhaps the best professionals in the field, that what I was seeing was real, that my instincts were correct.

Trauma Center at JRI, excerpt from the section titled Mental Status:

During this evaluation, Jason did not report intent to harm self or others. However, on a couple of occasions, he has reported to his mother that he does not want to be alive, and he has indicated to her that he does not have happy feelings. His parents' report of a significant shift in mood with a marked increase in irritability indicates that he is at risk for depression. Both parents' endorsements on questionnaires indicate clinical significance for both internalized and externalized symptoms, including depression, anxiety, anger, PTSD symptoms and dissociative symptoms. During this evaluation, Jason seemed to experience some range of emotion, but he consistently was unable or unwilling to report having feelings, which is unusual for a four-year-old child. He would not or could not name situations in which he felt happy, sad, mad or scared, eventually providing one example of feeling scared in a fun way. Each time the evaluator asked him about feelings, he quickly became active in taking control of the activity and of the conversation, drawing the faces himself, interviewing the evaluator, or scribbling over the faces. It will be important to provide opportunities in less pressured contexts for Jason to identify and express basic feelings.

Trauma Center at JRI, excerpt from the section titled Clinical Impressions:

One of the main concerns and reasons for the

referral for this evaluation, is the question of exposure to abuse, both because of his statements to his mother about his former nanny, and because of his behaviors and language.

Although Jason did not report abuse experiences in this evaluation, the possibility of exposures cannot be ruled out. The structured interview about touch provides the child with an opportunity to talk about certain experiences, but it is not an absolute test to rule out abuse. It is possible that Jason did not understand the questions or that he chose not to talk about certain experiences or that he tended to underreport negative experiences. It is notable that he stated he has never been hit; it is unusual for kids to have never been hit by siblings or other kids.

Jason's statements to his mother about his former nanny Carette spanking him and punching him in the stomach should be considered seriously. It is not uncommon for children to make statements to a parent before they are able to tell anyone else. Children may also tell only their parents since they do not necessarily feel the need to tell anyone else after they have reported events to the parent. In Jason's case, he no longer had contact with Carette and may not have felt the need to talk about her further. Additionally, young children tend to provide information over time, as they feel safe enough to do so, rather than in one initial narrative. Sometimes during this process they refute earlier statements. During this evaluation, Jason appeared uncomfortable when asked about

Carette, and was very reluctant to talk about her. He did say that of the babysitters or nannies that the family has used, he liked only one of them (the current one named Hannah) and that "Carette was the most one I hate" but that he forgot why. It is interesting that Jason named a feeling in relation to Carette, since, as noted above, he generally did not name feelings. When the evaluator referenced Jason's statements to his mother about Carette spanking and punching him, Jason avoided responding and seemed to shut down. He said he did not want to talk about it, asked to go to the bathroom, started yawning, made comments about the time and put his head on the table. During the following session, the evaluator again asked him to talk about Carette. Jason avoided eye contact, said he didn't want to talk about it and attempted to gain more control of the conversation by placing post-it notes with X's over the evaluator's notes, saying he was "covering up words" and doing it "Because I don't want to be talking about this." These behaviors and his demeanor were markedly different from the way he presented at other times during the session or generally over the course of five sessions.

The Bering's reports of Jason's sexualized behaviors should also be considered. Some kinds of sexual behavior by young children fall within a developmentally normal range; generally, behaviors that are within the context of exploration and curiosity are to be expected and are considered part of normal, healthy development. Behaviors that are cause for concern are behaviors that the child does not stop when adults set limits, that are secretive, that cause shame in the child or in others, that feel coercive or aggressive to others, or that occupy disproportionate amount of the child's time and energy. (See Toni Cavanagh Johnson.) Jason's behaviors are concerning because they feel aggressive to his parents and because he does not respond to their interventions. It is noted that Jason has directed these behaviors only to his parents, and mostly to his mother, and not to other children.

Jason's recent use of language when he is angry or distressed is notable. It is concerning that there is not a clear source for where or from whom he learned some words. Some words are what many children might say when angry (fart, butt) but others are not easily explained outside of a context of abuse or exposure.

It does seem that there is a confluence of several issues and conditions within the family. Both parents reported longstanding dissension in their marriage that increased during the past year, and it is likely that Jason has been affected by this tension. One source of marital tension was the revelation that as a child, Mr. Bering had engaged in a sexually inappropriate relationship with his younger sister. Ms. Bering made a few out of town trips during the past year, therefore Jason was separated from her for significant periods for the first time. A sensitive temperament would make it more difficult to cope with either of these stressors or with a babysitter yelling at or being mean to him or giving him many time-outs. Finally, Jason seems to have difficulty identifying and expressing basic emotions, and therefore he might be relying on behaviors to express them.

Trauma Center at JRI, excerpt from section titled Family History:

Mr. Bering reported a personal history of sexual contact with his sister that he initiated when he was thirteen years old and his sister was ten. He related that neither of them received help at the time. Mr. Bering noted that he does not remember very much about his childhood. A caseworker at the Alaska Office of Child Services (OCS) told this evaluator that there was a report to that office in August 2009 about the sexual contact between the siblings, that the age of the siblings was reported as fifteen and thirteen, and that a four-year-old sister was also reportedly involved. The identity of the reporter to OCS is confidential. The report was screened out because of the historic nature of the information, and because the reported events did not occur in the jurisdiction of Alaska (they occurred in Massachusetts).

There was no notation in the Trauma Center report, questioning Cal's admission. *Why didn't they look further into Cal's history of molesting his sisters? Was there a connection to Jason's symptoms?* My disappointment turned to grief when my family's only recourse offered by one of the most reputable trauma care facilities in the world was a report with a list of recommendations. I was ready to relocate for his care. I had the financial resources, *and* the willingness to relocate for Jason's continuity of care and intervention, yet, my urgency was ignored.

Turmoil

Compassion is not a relationship between the healer and the wounded. It's a relationship between equals. Only when we know our own darkness well, can we be present with the darkness of others. Compassion becomes real when we recognize our shared humanity.

Pema Chödrön

In cognitive therapy during late fall of 2010 and early winter of 2011, Jason benefitted from Sophia's wisdom. She was an experienced therapist who worked with him and taught me how to work with him. These one-hour-long therapy sessions were some of the only times that I could relax during the week, because a trained eye was observing behaviors in my child that I was otherwise alone with.

I said to her, "If my son were an adult, he would be medicated. What can you recommend for him?"

She answered, "A calm and loving environment."

That prescription required a lot of patience, creativity, and diligence.

She taught me how to respond and gave me things that I could do to help calm him. When I lamented, "My baby has been stolen from me," she reassured me he had been "hijacked" not "stolen." Her words gave me hope that if he were "hijacked" he would one day be restored.

I did exercises to promote eye contact between my son and me, to help rebuild trust and connection and to pull him into the present moment. We swung him in a sheet turned into a hammock, while looking him in the eye and singing to him, to help calm his nervous system and to prevent him from dissociating while he absorbed a sense of calm and well-being. I thought to myself, *I can work with "hi-jacked." I can love this child as much as is humanly possible and teach him that he is safe and that certain people can be trusted.*

We watched week after week as Jason used puzzle pieces to illustrate physical violence and then he hid the pieces under the couch or in the trash. He blackened out happy faces and said he did not recognize those feelings at all. He consistently chose the book where the mom went away but said she would be back.

We were four months into this therapy, when one day I walked into an appointment with a letter in my hand. Clara had been conditionally accepted to Phillips Andover Academy, pending the release of the semester's grades.

I put the letter down on the window sill by the therapist's blue couch. I said to her, "If you need me to be a part of therapy with Jason in order for it to continue, then we're going to have to stop meeting for a while. Jason's sister, Clara, revealed to me that her father has been abusing her since her earliest memories in childhood. I need to focus on Clara right now. But, I hope you will continue to treat Jason if I can't be here."

2

Getaway

True beauty in a woman is reflected in her soul.

Audrey Hepburn

My teenage daughter lay stretched out on her stomach in my bed, doing her homework. I had put a pillow over my eyes to block the light from her reading lamp. The warm sensation of her lying next to me filled my heart.

I had talked Cal into letting us go away together. He agreed to make arrangements for the two of us to get away to Seattle for a shopping weekend.

"Really, Mom?" She suddenly raised the pillow off my face, and I could see the joy on hers. "Yes! Let's go!"

At our first restaurant, Clara sat over a huge plate of gourmet food. She beamed with silly delight as we talked and laughed, enjoying the meal together. I was struck by her beauty and intelligence as we blithely chatted, her kindness as she so graciously thanked me for this special care. I would treasure every minute of this time alone with her.

The next evening, after a day of hiking and another great dinner, we got ready to settle into our room for the night.

"Honey," I began. "I hope you know you can talk to me about anything. You don't have to. But I am always here for you."

She kept her back to me, continuing to dial through radio stations, trying to find music that would suit us both. I lay on the fresh hotel sheets, my head propped up on the starchy pillows.

Her words floated across the room soft as a feather.

"Mom, you know when we got back from our trip to the east coast, and you asked me if Dad ever touched me inappropriately?"

The sage green paint on the ceiling tore free of the perfect white crown molding, as the sky began to fall. My body trembled, heart raced, stomach tightened. I willed my voice to steady itself.

"Yes. I remember." My heart tried to open to the searing scream of her silence. "You can talk to me about anything," I repeated, the words escaping calmly past the stranglehold her question had put on my larynx.

"You could talk to my health teacher," she said quietly.

The implications of what she was saying cut into me. I waited for several minutes before speaking.

"I don't need to go to your teacher. You can talk to me."

She whirled around, her fists at her side. "I will *not* talk to you! If you want to know, talk to my teacher!"

"Okay. Okay, Clara," I reassured her.

After some time passed, she came over and crawled into bed next to me. Big warm tears rolled down her soft, puffy cheeks.

"I am so disgusting," she sobbed.

"Who says you are disgusting?"

"The Bible."

Sobs. Warm tears. And the now rare sensation of holding her in my arms.

"I know that you are beautiful in the eyes of God."

Ms. Oceanhill

If you wanna fly, you got to give up that thing
that weighs you down.

Toni Morrison

When we had returned from our long weekend in Seattle in February 2011, I hit the ground with a mission to talk to Clara's health teacher. I said to my husband, "I need to contact Ms. Oceanhill so I can understand what is going on with Clara."

A wry, nervous smile appeared on his face. "I will talk to her; it'll be easier for me to stop over there on my way home." I agreed, recognizing I'd need to be home to attend to the boys. I would go talk to her later.

He reported that he'd told Ms. Oceanhill he was "addressing his issues." What those "issues" were exactly was still unclear to me. Were we talking about his past abuse of his sisters? Were we talking about the way our youngest child was acting out, which had consumed the energies of the family? Or were we talking about a recent vague and disturbing comment our daughter had made about her overachieving and perfectionism being a result of her father's actions?

I decided to go to see Ms. Oceanhill even though I was insecure and felt that it was not my position to discuss Clara's academics because Cal was much more qualified. But this was different now. I had come to some understandings that could not be reversed; we were not safe with Cal.

I discussed with Ms. Oceanhill how I wanted what was best for my daughter. I described some of the ways we'd been suffering over the years under Cal's continuing tyranny and explained that I was doing my best to manage the situation.

I told her I was so concerned for my daughter that I was in the process of trying to get her admitted to a boarding school on the east coast.

Ms. Oceanhill told me that, when she and Cal had talked earlier, she had encouraged him to turn himself in to the authorities for the past abuse of his siblings. He had convinced her that he was in counseling for his past behaviors and he was addressing the issues that had gone unchallenged in his adolescence. She could not believe that Cal had convinced her to trust him. She had thought she was too experienced to be conned.

As the conversation unfolded, Ms. Oceanhill informed me that Clara had not confirmed any abuse outright. She suspected it, though, based on Clara's overachieving and striving for perfection, as well as hints she'd been dropping.

Ms. Oceanhill was handling the situation delicately. Later, I came to appreciate her patient approach, recognizing that she made it possible for the truth to finally be brought to light.

This teacher could see the vulnerable child hiding under Clara's tough exterior. She was keeping my daughter safe by actively listening. She explained to me how she'd learned that reporting abuse prematurely yields no results.

Ms. Oceanhill then voiced concern about the potential for my husband to harm our other children. She said that when a predator feels stressed, he often escalates and resorts to more abuse. She was seeing a connection between Jason's behavior and Cal's abusive past. The stress Cal was under was making him more dangerous.

She also shared with me my daughter's concern that our family would land in poverty if legal consequences were imposed on her father. Ms. Oceanhill was aware of the injustices that await a family disrupted by legal and emotional costs when the criminal is the breadwinner.

This was the beginning of my relationship with Ms. Oceanhill. Up until then, my husband had taken it on himself to meet with Clara's teachers and oversee all of her academics.

I took Clara out to dinner after hearing Ms. Oceanhill's thoughts about what was going on. She sat over her favorite meal of steak and a soda. I tried to follow the teacher's modeling, asking Clara if she'd be willing to answer just three "yes" or "no" questions. She agreed.

"Was your father inappropriate with you?"

"Yes."

"Did he sexually abuse you?"

"Yes."

"Did this happen over a span of years?"

"Yes."

As we drove away from the restaurant, Clara implored me, "Mom, please don't be mean to Dad."

Aware her loyalty to her father was strong, I said, "He is a very sick man. I will not be mean to him, but things will change."

Running

Without saying a word, Clara and I put on our running clothes and step out into the dark winter evening.

The temperature is approaching sub-zero. We start down the street in the direction of the dike trail. We don't talk about the abuse. We laugh at the dog. We share a sense of humor decodable only by each other. We know how to keep it going, this laughing and silliness.

My girl is a nature lover. She wonders at the stars and fears nothing. I am always a little afraid of the dark and don't like standing in the cold night. After her suffering so much because of my failure to protect her, the least I can do is run in the dark with her. I am grateful she still wants me to. I feel like someone who did not step in to prevent a murder. But she is alive. We are alive.

We've covered our ears and hands and upper and lower bodies with coats and hats and gloves and tights and socks.

We jog around the end of the runway. On our right, the river plots its winding escape to the ocean. The path is all ice and frozen dirt. The smiling dog's sweet presence is our unity. I wonder to myself about his acquired wisdom; the silence he keeps amid all the trauma. He has always loved Clara so much, I sense his suffering for her suffering.

We turn the corner into the narrow forest, the airport on one side, tide flats stretching for two miles on the other. We run by a tree that we decorated one year with the neighbor. I ask, "Do you remember when we sat on the bank under the moon and drank thermoses of hot chocolate with all the kids?" I've asked *this too often for her to bother answering.*

Normally, this part of the trail would be blindingly dark, but something is being built, or at least improved, under flood lights that illuminate our way through the first part of the trees. Then, suddenly, nothing but darkness.

We know this trail by heart, but still when running it in the dark, it's impossible not to fear colliding with some waiting object—a bear. A new fence. A man. We turn around together and sprint back home.

"It's true."

The tables have turned, Larry. We have our voices;
and we are not going anywhere.

Aly Raisman
Victim Impact Statement
Larry Nassar's Sentence Hearing

After Shelley told me about Cal's past abuse, I had asked him to start sleeping in the spare bedroom. Now, knowing he'd molested Clara, I asked him to move to a mat on the floor next to my bed. I needed to know exactly where he was.

The night after my dinner with Clara, I got child care, so I could take Cal out and talk with him about what I had learned. I sat across from him, confused, a fly struggling in a web. Tears overflowed my eyes.

"Please," I said, "please don't let this be true—that you sexually abused our daughter."

His dry, thin lips smiled nervously. "It's true," he said.

I couldn't hold back my outrage. "She's your child. Her body is hers. It is your job to protect her. I mean . . . she's power, purity. Strength. Beauty. She's amazing. She's stunning and brilliant. How could you put all that aside and let yourself do this? Were you attracted to her sexually?"

"Yes."

"Did you ever touch her body?"

"I moved the sheets so I could see her better . . . and I

121

masturbated while I looked at her body. I *was* like a pedophile. But I'm not anymore. I'm cured. I think I had a demon. But the demon's left me, now." He paused. "I stole from you."

I looked at him. I had no idea what he was talking about.

"You were trusting and kind."

An anger welled up in me so powerful my body wanted to turn itself inside out. There was nothing I could ever do to right this wrong. The years. The lost innocence. The broken trust. He degraded the trust of his wife and then, the unimaginable, his own child. Anger is not a strong enough word to describe the combination of disillusionment, betrayal, and disgust his actions brought up in me.

The day after my conversation with Cal, my good friend Stella was concerned about me. She encouraged me to stop by her house. I stood in her doorway.

"Come in."

"I can't. It isn't good."

"It's Clara, isn't it?"

"I can't say."

I looked down. Tears dropped out of my eyes, splashing onto the metal threshold of her doorway

"It isn't good."

She looked at me. I didn't want to be there. Or anywhere. She walked me into her sunlit porch. I sat on her black leather couch.

"What's going on?"

"It *is* Clara. Something happened. I don't know what he did, but something happened. I can't believe this. I can't believe this. I'm so sorry. I'm so sorry I missed it. I'm so sorry I missed it. I'm so sorry I missed it."

For the next month, I left gifts and notes on Clara's pillow. I cleaned her room. I cried so hard that my eyes swelled shut for days. All I could say, out loud and in my head, was "I'm sorry sweetheart. I'm sorry sweetheart. I'm sorry. I'm so, so sorry."

Nothing touched the pain. Nothing.

Clarity

We are searchlights, we see in the dark
We are rockets, pointed up at the stars
We are billions of beautiful hearts
And you sold us down the river too far

Pink
"What About Us"

In the following period of information explosion, friends surrounded me and my children to comfort, advise, counsel, and direct. These friends, who had celebrated many life events with us and helped us through difficulties in our marriage, were now there for me and the children. My two closest friends, Stella and Kayla, sat at my kitchen table, just to be a presence in my home while Cal was still not incarcerated or removed from the family.

Inside of a week's time, I had talked over our situation with the Cranes, a couple from our church who I viewed as spiritual mentors. They counseled me to try to work things out with my husband in counseling—to save the marriage. This did not sit well with me for innumerable reasons. They wanted me to isolate the information and work with them and my husband. It was a rich offer—that they were willing to deal with such a dark issue and all the problems associated with a family impacted by pedophilia. They offered to be present for me when my husband minimized or did not validate my devastation (which was all he did), so that, too, was an incredible burden to offer to carry with me. They wanted me to work on my marriage to maintain the structure for the younger children. I knew this would totally negate my promise to Clara, and to myself, to help her recover from the abuse. With Cal in the house, there would be no way I would be able to ensure the safety of my children.

Working on my marriage at this point would be like trying to put the mushroom cloud over Hiroshima back into the bombshell. Relying on anyone to keep my husband accountable and teach him how to care? Amid all the turmoil, one thing that became and stayed clear to me was that Cal lacked any capacity to care. There was no marriage. I told the Cranes that I appreciated their generosity but make no mistake: there was *nothing* to be saved or made whole.

The Cranes were encouraging me to stay for religious reasons. I was revolted by this response. Predators hide in settings where people offer compassion and kindness. There is no love without justice. Compassion is sending a predator to jail.

Cal was trying to figure out his next moves for damage control. He was meeting with the Cranes, too. Stella was meeting with the Cranes and Cal, because Mr. Crane had been calling my cell phone non-stop trying to get me to reconcile with Cal. I stopped answering his call. Mr. Crane then reached out to Stella and was calling her non-stop until she agreed to meet with them. Mr. and Mrs. Crane were harassing Stella, trying to get her to convince me to forgive Cal and take him back. They laid out all the reasons that pursuing this with police would go badly for me and my family and how Cal was a changed man.

"Don't you believe God changes people?" Mr. Crane asked Stella

Cal was sitting with the Cranes and he said, "You know pedophiles never get convicted."

Finally, back at her car, Stella found a note from Cal in her driver's seat that said, "Thank you for praying for my family."

Other friends stepped in and held me up. It was hell on them, too, as they came to realize that my daughter, the girl they'd known and loved for so long, the girl they had watched grow into a wonderful teenager, had suffered sexual abuse—at the hands of the man they thought they knew. He had fooled everyone.

It all happened so quickly; many conversations were happening at once. Another close friend, Jenelle, said to me, "You have 24 hours to report, or I will."

Cal immediately wanted to talk Jenelle out of it: "Put me on the phone with her," he demanded.

It did not work.

Overnight Cal became fiercely religious. He donated nearly a thousand dollars to the church. He went on a men's retreat that was occurring imminently, that weekend, with the church. He tried hard to create a cushion of support in the last moments before the truth of his double life undid him.

Jenelle counseled me, "If a father even glances at his daughter in a sexual way, it can have lifelong consequences for the child."

Frightened and shaky, I stood in front of Cal, the man that had been my partner for 20 years, and looked into his eyes.

"You have to leave the house," I told him.

His eyes darkened like inkwells. He said, "You are my wife. You have to support me."

I said "I don't understand what you have done. You have to leave."

I hid under my pillow and cried as he grabbed his belongings.

"Can I sleep in the car in the driveway?"

"No. That would be too hard on the kids."

He went through the house grabbing his belongings and I don't know what. It seemed like forever before I heard the telltale sound of the old windows rattling, as they did every time the back door closed. The familiar pounding of his heavy footsteps as he dropped down the old back porch adjacent to our backyard, past the zipline, the tree fort with attached swing and past the partially completed log cabin fort that he was building with the boys.

He started up his old black truck and drove off.

Moment of Truth

When people are free to choose, they choose freedom.

Margaret Thatcher

Three of us have gathered in my family's beautiful home, with its hardwood floors that Cal and his former boss and best friend installed, the cozy woodstove, recently renovated kitchen with cast iron pans hanging over the gas stove, and the children's nearby bedrooms and bathroom. Clara's teacher, Ms. Oceanhill, sits in a chair in the corner of the living room. Near her, Jenelle has settled into the cozy leather couch.

My healthy, smart, strong, 15-year-old daughter climbs the stairs from her bedroom, and announces to us, "I'm glad you are all here. But I am not going to say anything." She then takes her seat next to me on the couch.

Since the day she was born, I have been in awe of the raw power my daughter projects. Sitting next to her now, I try to reconcile the fact of that power with the emerging truths of her stolen childhood. It's like trying to mix rocks and orange juice in a blender. My brain feels like that container, about to shatter.

I keep seeing Clara as a nine-year-old, in her yellow and black bathing suit, running through the sprinkler with her little brother—her wide smile, her adult-sized teeth too big for her little face. I can hear her laughter as I watch her running through the sprinkler's chilling rain—as if somehow that image of a happy child might neutralize the acid reality burning my heart.

I thought that I had protected my child by staying with her father. I thought that I had made the best possible choice for her success in life. Because who loves and protects a child more than her own father? In my mistaken mind, the answer to this question was the driver behind every choice that I made. Every effort that I had put forth to make my marriage stable and workable was based on the belief that he, and us as a unit, were her best chance for success. I was wrong. Irreparably wrong.

The exploitation of our family had been finely executed by the father of my children. Nuances like a strained mother-daughter relationship, which is generally considered normal, were being twisted just enough to suffocate us slowly. I was told *I* was abnormal for caring so much about my relationship with my daughter, that our issues were prevalent in all homes. The degree to which I suffered and sought help for my family, this was the same degree that I was considered disturbed and our problems considered to be of my invention. All the while, all those years, I had walked around with a lump in my throat, wanting to scream, "IT'S NOT NORMAL!" But I couldn't explain why. I just didn't know why. I had been unable to discern the truth.

The man who posed as my husband saw our stunning daughter as his protégé. My memories now provided a bit of ground on which to get a foothold. So much was beginning to make sense. The realization of the abuse answered questions that had been eating at me on a cellular level for a long time. There existed in the past a palpable resistance. Cal did nothing to engage with the needs of our family unless it suited him. He maintained this authoritative posture throughout our marriage, while I dug deep to find some way to improve our home situation and the lives of our children.

With Cal gone, our home life quickly began to repair itself. My daughter was hurt, but alive, and sitting next to me now, amid three women determined to protect her, inviting her trust.

Ms. Oceanhill asks, "Do you want to talk about anything?"

Clara shakes her head, "No."

"Are you willing to share with us any concerns or heaviness that you are carrying?"

Clara shakes her head, "No."

Ms. Oceanhill then asks me, "Do you have anything that you want to say?"

"I don't want him going directly to Clara to ask her what she remembers, to try to find out what she plans to report," I respond.

Clara turns to me. "Dad said you wanted me to tell him what I remember from the abuse. He wanted me to write it all down."

"When?" I was confused.

"A while back. When you went to Florida for the marathon? He came to me and said you wanted me to tell him everything I remembered about the abuse."

I shake my head. "No. I'm sorry, Clara. I never asked him to do that? Why would I? I had no idea what he was doing . . . I wouldn't have left you with him . . ."

She stands up. "I realize now what he was up to."

She realizes it all. She's known better than any of us his lies, the double life. As would later become known, she has withstood his interrogations on excruciatingly long car rides, listened to him ask himself moral questions he'd already decided to sidestep:

"When do you think I should tell Mom?"

"I'm going to wait until you graduate from high school."

"No. I'm going to wait until you are in college."

"I'm not sure that I am going to say anything to Mom at all."

She learned that if she did not respond, he'd turn the car back toward home that much sooner.

She would later tell me how, during one of these rides, she'd blurted out in frustration, "Tell her when you want to tell her, but don't fuck up my life!"

"He needs to go to treatment," she now says to me and the other two women. "And not just a slap on the wrist treatment. He needs serious treatment."

Up to that night, we had yet to learn the details of what her life had been like—the secrets she had been coerced to keep, some of them so horrible she would choose never to unbury them.

The meeting ends with an understanding that Ms. Oceanhill would report the abuse the next day.

I called my parents to let them know what was going on. My father's words: "Darling, I'm sorry. At this point, it's out of your control."

My mother said simply, "We don't know him."

The man who posed as my husband said that he called his mother to tell her what was going on. I asked, "What did she say?"

He said: "She feels like she betrayed her granddaughter. She said she would pay for me to go to the treatment facility that Tiger Woods went to. I offered for us to take out a loan."

"You are on your own with that one, Cal. I am not taking out a loan to bear the costs of your criminal behavior."

The next morning, after running the wetlands trail in the bright sun with a friend, I stood in the shower. I held the phone in my hand, trying to keep the falling water from destroying it.

I had a detective from the police department on one line and my husband calling me from work on the other.

"You have to deal with your treatment. But I don't think it's going to be up to you for too much longer," I informed him.

He promptly left work and went to the office of the best criminal attorney in town—the lawyer people always said to go to if you were "in deep shit."

He called me from his attorney's office: "I can't talk to you anymore. You have to get an attorney."

"For what?" I had no idea why I would need an attorney. But I did as he suggested. I called the number I had written on the duct tape that held my Bible together—a number I'd scribbled down recently for a local divorce attorney.

Now, in addition to the teacher reporting the abuse, my daughter made the decision that she was going to give a full report to the police. But she was leaving on a school trip with the chorus and, because of her age, the department needed more time to get its investigative team together.

In the meantime, Cal began to text me relentlessly, begging me to talk to him. Assuring me "he was now ready to be the husband I had always wanted."

His frantic words scared me. My attorney advised me to ignore the pleas. "Why would you talk to him? You are working with the police. Are you going to lie to him?"

Fearful of ignoring him, I resolved to arrange a group meeting in a public area.

"I will meet with you in a public area," I told him. "I am not going to say anything. I am just going to listen. And, I am going to have two friends with me."

We met on a breezy Monday, in the early afternoon, after Cal got off work. There is a nice little picnic area near the docks where huge cruise ships carried tourists exploring Alaska's vast beauty. Behind us was the channel, the boardwalk where locals enjoy a stroll on their lunch hour and where tourists can enjoy a panoramic mountain view. To our left is the Wharf where local eating spots and bars attract locals and tourists, to the right of us is the downtown high rise containing a library and a parking deck, and off of the docks is the landing zone for small, chartered aircrafts.

Stella and Tim, both of whom had been my close friends for years, were with me. I wore dark sunglasses because I didn't want him to look into my eyes. I was no longer devoted to him. I was now devoted to protecting my child and uncovering the truth of who I had married.

We sat at a square table surrounded by four benches, so we each had our own bench to sit on. It wasn't quite tourist season yet, so all the pedestrian traffic was local. As we were congregating around the table, I saw my husband heading our way, dressed in khaki pants and blue button-down shirt, the wind blowing his wavy hair. Cal blithely jogged over from the direction of the state office buildings which were located up the hill on Main street, opposite the docks.

It felt strange to observe him from a distance—this man I'd always been so proud of now prompted an intense nausea to rise from the pit of my stomach. He looked at me, mildly amused that I had sunglasses on, but realizing that he was no longer in the intimate partnership that allowed him to make a comment on my appearance.

The chemistry at this table was clearly one where he was disconnected from the three of us. Not so much because we had disconnected from him, but he had disconnected from us. His demeanor was reserved, yet buoyant, as he maintained composure and control.

We opened the conversation with prayer. Tim is a member of the clergy, and prayer was a big part of the lives of all of us in this outdoor meeting. I had told my friends and my husband that I was not going to say anything. This turned out fine as Cal proceeded to do all the talking.

Tim and Stella looked on sincerely as he spoke.

"I want to go over the elements of the crime with my daughter because I don't want her to think that she is crazy. I don't want any of you driving the punishment behind the crimes that I committed. I want my daughter to decide what she thinks is necessary. If she thinks that I should serve 25 years, then that is what I will do. And if she wants me around to support the family... I want that to be her decision. Not yours." As he said this, he looked around the table at each one of us individually.

The conversation went on for a short while longer and then closed in prayer. It became evident during the discussion, or monologue, that he was incapable of understanding the nature of his affliction.

Tim exhaled pensively as we watched Cal walk back in the direction of the state office building. "He is a very sick man."

I hugged Tim. "Thank you for being here."

On the car ride home with Stella, I called the detective.

"Can you get a wiretap to record a conversation?"

Consequences

Dad, you can't make things right without being honest.

Clara

After I hung up from talking with the detective, I began to think back on my husband's and my relationship. For most of our years together it had not felt right. I saw now I had been nothing more to Cal than a woman to produce children for him to dominate. Pretty, social, and with a strong instinct to keep my family together, I had provided him with the cover he needed. My desire to heal our family had been so strong that it had enabled him to string me along while putting little effort into the marriage.

In late 2011, the book *Truth or Consequences: Life inside the Madoff Family* came out and was being promoted through media appearances by Bernard Madoff's son, Andrew.

I recognized some of our struggle in the words of this man who had been used by his dad for financial gain: "One of the hardest things to come to grips with in trying to get my head around this was that feeling that I had been used almost as a human shield by him. It's unforgivable. No father should do that," Andrew told CBS News.

He described the way his father had sobbed when he told his sons about the fraud. At one point, Andrew had draped his arm around his father and cried, too, before the brothers went to their lawyers and authorized them to report the fraud to authorities. Andrew explained his conflicted emotions at the time: "I would love to say that Mark and I were waving the flags of justice in the air, but the bottom line is that we were absolutely terrified. We knew that what we were doing was going to send our father to jail, and the feeling was awful—absolutely awful."

What this adult child of Mr. Madoff described about his and his brother's pain at turning their father in to the authorities drew me closer to understanding fully the bravery of my 15-year-old daughter as she turned *her* father into the authorities.

What her father had done was inexcusable. However, the child was not waving the flag of justice in the air; she was terrified. She knew that by telling the truth she would be sending her father to jail.

Clara exited the undercover police car that escorted her from the high school to the police station. Her black Converse All Star sneakers carried her wiry 15-year-old frame, topped with a long blonde ponytail, through the large, shiny Police Department doors, through another door without a window, down a hallway to a room where a wire was taped to her soft skin. Moments later she was transported to the towering local library to record the conversation that would send her abuser to jail.

The plainclothes officers instructed her, "We are giving you a soda bottle. If at any time you feel threatened, take the bottle cap off the soda bottle, and we will interrupt the meeting."

The Alaska Constitution requires police to obtain a warrant prior to the surreptitious seizure (by recording) of a conversation. This is commonly referred to as a "Glass warrant," after the court case that established it.

INITIAL CONTACT WITH FATHER- ~ 2:15PM [SEVERAL VOICES]
[TALK ABOUT MUSIC FEST AND SOME CLOTHES CHILD BOUGHT]
CHILD: I WAS UNDER THE IMPRESSION YOU WANTED TO MEET TO TALK TO ME ABOUT THINGS YOU REMEMBER. IS THAT ACCURATE?
FATHER: NO. I WANTED TO TALK ABOUT THINGS I DON'T REMEMBER THAT I THINK, UM I WANT YOU TO FEEL, I WANT YOU TO KNOW I'M [?] ABOUT EVERYTHING THAT UM THAT THE THINGS THAT YOU'RE TALKING ABOUT HAPPENED HAPPENED ...COULD NOT BELIEVED IT...AND ME NOT HAVING A CONCRETE MEMORY IM SURE MOST LIKELY PROTECTIVE OF MYSELF...THAT I COULDN'T THAT I DID SUCH HORRIBLE THINGS. SO I TRULY BELIEVE YOU FIRST OFF. AND THEN I, I DO HAVE MEMORIES ENOUGH, OR NOT MEMORIES, I HAVE LIKE LITTLE LIKE TEXTURES IN MY MIND THAT I DON'T CALL MEMORIES BECAUSE THERE IS NO BEGINNING OR END OR MID, THERE'S ... TO ME THEY'RE CONFUSING CAUSE I DON'T KNOW IF I THOUGHT THEM OR DID 'EM OR
CHILD: WAIT. WHEN YOU SAY YOU FULLY, WHY DID YOU SAY YOU FULLY AGREE WITH EVERYTHING I SAY?
FATHER: I FULLY BELIEVE YOU...NONE OF ME IS DENYING WHAT YOU'RE SAYING.
CHILD: OK
FATHER: I WANT TO BE CLEAR. I'M NOT DENYING ANYTHING THAT YOU SAY.
CHILD: SO, YOU'RE NOT DENYING THAT LIKE YOU WOULD HAVE TOUCHED ME INAPPROPRIATELY LIKE?
FATHER: YEAH
CHILD: TOUCHED ME ON THE VAGINA, NOT PENETRATION THAT LIKE

FATHER: I DON'T KNOW ABOUT THE VAGINA, BUT THAT AREA DOWN THERE

CHILD: OK

FATHER: THE VAGINA

CHILD: SO YOU'RE SAYING YOU DON'T REMEMBER IT BUT YOU AGREE IT COULD HAVE HAPPENED?

FATHER: WELL [?] TRY TO FLESH THAT OUT MORE

CHILD: OK

FATHER: NO PUN INTENDED. UM BECAUSE I DO REMEMBER WANTING TO PUT MY HAND DOWN THERE.

CHILD: YES

FATHER: AND I REMEMBER PUTTING IT ON YOUR STOMACH AND PUTTING IT UNDERNEATH YOUR UNDERWEAR, I JUST DON'T EVER REMEMBER GETTING TO THE POINT WHERE I TOUCHED ANYTHING, AND MY, I'M THINKING THAT YOU WERE SO YOUNG THAT BASICALLY IT FELT JUST LIKE A CONTINUATION OF YOUR STOMACH. THERE WOULD HAVE BEEN NO HAIR, WOULD BE NO, SO MY MEMORY, I DO REMEMBER REMEMBER PUTTING MY HAND ON YOUR STOMACH AND I REMEMBER THINKING ABOUT DOING IT, I JUST DON'T REMEMBER GETTING TO THE POINT OF ACTUALLY TOUCHING IT. SO IT'S KIND OF LIKE, I DID IT, OK?

CHILD: OK.

FATHER: I'M NOT SAYING I DIDN'T.

CHILD: OK

FATHER: WHEN I SAY I DON'T' REMEMBER IT, IT'S CAUSE I DON'T ACTUALLY REMEMBER TOUCHING THE SPOT. I JUST REMEMBER, I REMEMBER WANTING TO, I REMEMBER STARTING TO, I JUST DON'T REMEMBER THAT FACT THAT I ACTUALLY DID SO

CHILD: THAT DOESN'T MAKE ANY SENSE. YOU DO UNDERSTAND THAT DOESN'T MAKE ANY SENSE, RIGHT? LIKE WHEN YOU HEAR YOURSELF SAY THAT, IT REALLY DOES NOT MAKE ANY SENSE TO ANYONE THAT YOU COULD REMEMBER EVERYTHING LEADING TO IT, BUT NOT THE ACTUAL MOLESTATION?

FATHER: I DO. I'M SURE IT'S, THAT'S WHAT I SAID, IT'S PROBABLY EITHER BLOCKING IT OUT, IT'S, I MEAN I DON'T KNOW IF YOU, WHAT YOU REMEMBER, BUT I DON'T EVER REMEMBER, UM

CHILD: WHY WOULD YOU BE BLOCKING IT OUT?

FATHER: CAUSE I MOLESTED MY DAUGHTER. WHY WOULDN'T I? I MEAN THAT'S THE WORST THING A FATHER CAN DO.

CHILD: OK. SO WHAT'S YOUR PURPOSE IN THIS CONVERSATION? AND I'M A LITTLE BIT CONFUSED. BECAUSE...

FATHER: I WANTED TO SAY, I WANTED TO GO THROUGH SOME OF MY MEMORIES TO CONFIRM, VERIFY

CHILD: OK

FATHER: CORROBORATE YOUR BELIEF. BECAUSE I DON'T WANT YOU FEELING LIKE I DON'T BELIEVE IT HAPPENED AND I DON'T BELIEVE I NEED TO HAVE SOME LEVEL OF TREATMENT AND I DON'T NEED TO, AND THAT YOUR, YOU NEED TO KNOW THAT I KNOW WHAT I DID. I KNOW IT'S HORRIBLE. AND I KNOW THAT YOU ARE SUFFERING BECAUSE OF IT. AND YOU HAVE SUFFERED. THAT YOU'VE, THAT THERE'S NOTHING THAT COULD BE MORE CONFUSING TO A KID THAN TO HAVE THE DAD THAT WHEN THE LIGHTS AREN'T OUT IS LOVING AND, WELL, TRYING TO BE LOVING, BUT SUPPORTIVE

AND PROTECTING YOU AND THEN WHEN THE LIGHTS GO OUT I AM TREATING YOU WITH, AS A SEXUAL OBJECT.

CHILD: YOU KNOW THAT YOUR PROTECTIVE BEHAVIORS ARE GROOMING BEHAVIORS?

FATHER: A GROOMING?

CHILD: GROOMING. YES. GROOMING AS IN THEY'RE WHAT A PREDATOR DOES. IN TERMS OF LIKE THE OBSESSION WITH MY APPEARANCE.

FATHER: YEAH. I KNOW. I GO BACK AN LOOK AT IT. BUT I DON'T, I NEVER CONTEMPLATED OR ANYTHING EVER DOING ANYTHING TO YOU WHEN YOU WERE NOT ASLEEP AND I NEVER WOULD HAVE DONE ANYTHING TO YOU IF I KNEW YOU WERE AWAKE. AND YOU SHOULD BE ABLE TO REMEMBER THAT THE ROOFIE INCIDENT, WHICH WAS OVER THREE YEARS AGO NOW. WHEN I CAME INTO YOUR ROOM

CHILD: THE ROOFIE INCIDENT? IS THAT WHAT YOU CALLED IT?

FATHER: THE ROOFIE INCIDENT. THE TIME WHEN I

CHILD: YOU WERE ROOFIED?

FATHER: YEAH. THE TIME WHEN I, WELL THAT'S WHEN MY MALE CO-WORKERS AND I BELIEVE, WE ALL

CHILD: YOU GUYS ALL THINK THAT YOU WERE ROOFIED?

FATHER: IT'S A LONG STORY, IT'S IRRELEVANT. YOU CAN JUST CALL IT DRUNK.

CHILD: WHYYYY WOULD THE THREE OF YOU GUYS HAVE BEEN ROOFIED?

FATHER: IT'S A LONG STORY. IT'S IRRELEVANT TO THIS STORY.

CHILD: OK. SO WHEN YOU CAME IN AND YOU WERE ROOFIED

FATHER: AND I BOUNCED AND I LIKE HIT THE WALL AND I CAME IN AND I TOUCHED YOUR STOMACH AND THEN YOU TOLD ME THE NEXT DAY, YOU TOLD MOM, AND YOU TOLD ME THE NEXT DAY. THAT WAS THE FIRST TIME

CHILD: I DON'T REMEMBER TELLING YOU.

FATHER: YOU TOLD MOM, SHE TOLD ME YOU WERE UPSET. I TALKED TO YOU.

CHILD: OK

FATHER: THAT WAS THE FIRST TIME I EVER KNEW THAT YOU WERE AWAKENED BY ME AND I NEVER WENT IN YOUR ROOM AGAIN AFTER THAT.

CHILD: YES. I REMEMBER THAT.

FATHER: AND I WAS, I WAS NOT, SO I, DIDN'T COME HERE TO, UM

CHILD: OK

FATHER: I DIDN'T COME HERE TO DEFEND MYSELF. I'M JUST TRYING TO GIVE YOU AN IDEA THAT WHEN YOU

CHILD: I UNDERSTAND WHAT YOU'RE SAYING IS "I DIDN'T MEAN TO HURT YOU." BUT YOU DO REALIZE THAT IT'S EQUALLY FUCKED UP TO MOLEST SOMEONE IN THEIR SLEEP, RIGHT?

FATHER: YEAH. IT'S PROBABLY MORE

CHILD: BUT THAT DOESN'T ACTUALLY MAKE IT ANY BETTER, IN FACT IT KIND OF MAKES IT WORSE?

FATHER: YEAH

CHILD: BECAUSE THAT'S LIKE MASSIVELY CREEPY.

FATHER: I DO. I TOTALLY UNDERSTAND THAT. SO I'M NOT SAYING IT'S LESS OR MORE, I'M JUST SAYING LIKE IT WAS NEVER GOING TO GO DOWN THE PATH OF...SAY WHERE ONE GROOMS SOMEONE SO THEY CAN HAVE SEXUAL RELATIONS LIKE

CHILD: YES

FATHER: CONSCIOUS SEXUAL RELATIONS

CHILD: YES

FATHER: THAT. UM, WHEN WE WERE IN MAINE AND DID SEX ED TALK WITH YOU THAT, UM, SO YOU WOULD HAVE BEEN LIKE 9.

CHILD: IN MAINE? I WAS NOT 9 IN MAINE DAD!

FATHER: HOW OLD WERE YOU IN MAINE?

CHILD: IN MAINE I WOULD HAVE BEEN 7 AND 8.

FATHER: OK. SO YOU WERE 8. WE WERE TALKING ABOUT SEX ED AND ... THIS WAS THE FIRST TIME I WAS AWAKENED TO THE FACT THAT YOU WERE GOING TO BE SEXUAL, A SEXUAL BEING AND I WAS, UM IT WAS LIKE, IT WAS, I, IT WAS THE BEGINNING OF ME THINKING OF YOU AS, LIKE, WHAT WAS GOING TO BE. WHAT YOU WERE GOING TO BECOME. WHEN WE WENT ON OUR HAWAII TRIP, THEN YOU WERE 10. UM, WE STAYED IN YOUR UNCLE'S ROOM. AND YOU AND ME AN MOM SLEPT IN THE SAME BED. AND I WAS DRUNK AND I BELIEVED THAT I TOUCHED YOU THAT NIGHT. BUT MOM WAS IN BED NEXT TO ME AND SO I HAD TOLD HER THIS. I SAID THAT'S THE TIME I MOST THINK I DID. BUT I DON'T KNOW BECAUSE SHE WAS IN BED TOO, AND I WAS DRUNK AND IT WAS LIKE, THERE WERE JUST KIND OF BODIES ALL OVER. BUT I THINK I DID. AND THEN I START, UH, BE CHANGING IN YOUR ROOM, AND HAVE MY CLOTHES IN YOUR ROOM, AND I'D TAKE MY SHOWERS AND I'D COME IN YOUR ROOM NAKED AND YOU WERE AT THE AGE WHEN MY SISTER, WHO WAS ASLEEP, I WOULD COME IN AND LOOK AT HER BODY AND MASTURBATE. AND I DIDN'T THINK I WAS HURTING YOU. AND I WOULD, IF I THOUGHT I WAS HURTING YOU, I WOULDN'T'VE DONE IT. AND IF, I COULD'VE HURT YOU I WOULDN'T HAVE DONE IT. IF MY SISTER HAD SAID SOMETHING TO ME TO SAY, "YOU KNOW, I KNEW YOU WERE IN THERE AND IT FREAKED THE HECK OUT OF ME," I WOULD'VE NEVER DONE IT. I JUST THOUGHT I WAS GETTING AWAY WITH STUFF.

CHILD: DON'T YOU UNDERSTAND THE VICTIM MENTALITY AT ALL? I MEAN YOU'RE NOT A STUPID GUY. DON'T YOU UNDERSTAND WHAT IT WOULD TAKE FOR A YOUNG GIRL TO SAY, "DAD, I KNOW YOU HAVE HAD FREAKY SEXUAL URGES TOWARDS ME." I MEAN, I DON'T SEE HOW YOU CAN RATIONALIZE THAT IF YOU HAD ONLY KNOWN THAT IT WAS HURTING ME OR HURTING YOUR SISTER THAT YOU WOULDN'T HAVE DONE IT. BECAUSE YOU SHOULD HAVE KNOWN THAT IT WAS UN, UNHEALTHY BEHAVIOR. AND YOU SHOULD HAVE KNOWN THAT I COULD HAVE PLAUSIBLY BEEN AWAKE AT TIMES. AND WHAT WAS I GOING TO DO? HOW OFTEN DO KIDS

FATHER: HONEY, DO YOU THINK THAT I WAS THINKING CLEARLY?! I THOUGHT

CHILD: YOU WEREN'T DRUNK. WHAT WAS WRONG WITH YOUR HEAD?

FATHER: I, IT, IT'S I UNDERSTAND IT SOUNDS CRAZY, BUT I NEVER THOUGHT THAT I WAS, THAT YOU WERE GONNA, THAT YOU WERE AWAKE OR THAT YOU WERE EVEN GOING TO NOTICE, CAUSE I HAD DONE IT TO MY SISTER AND SHE NEVER WOKE UP. AND WHEN I TOLD HER, I TOLD HER THAT I DID IT WHEN SHE WAS COLLEGE AGE OR HIGH SCHOOL, AND SHE THANKED ME FOR TELLING HER AND SHE NEVER ACKNOWLEDGED THAT I HAD DONE IT. SHE NEVER SAID, "I KNEW THAT". I SAID 'I'M SORRY THAT I DID THIS, YOU PROBABLY NEVER KNEW, BUT I DID.' SHE NEVER SAID THAT AND IN RETROSPECT IT IS CRAZY. I AM A SMART PERSON. I SHOULD HAVE REALIZED, BUT I DIDN'T. I DON'T KNOW HOW DEEPLY PEOPLE SLEEP AND I, IT WAS SOMETHING THAT I DID AND I JUST THOUGHT THAT I WAS GETTING AWAY WITH IT AND

CHILD: WELL, SEE, THERE'S SOMETHING, THERE'S SOMETHING VERY DISTURBING ABOUT THE, JUST THAT YOU WERE GETTING AWAY WITH IT AND SO IT WAS OK, BECAUSE THERE'S A LOT OF THINGS THAT PEOPLE COULD THINK THEY ARE GETTING AWAY WITH. SO IF THAT'S YOUR MENTALITY. THAT IT'S OKAY IF YOU GET AWAY WITH IT, THEN THAT'S PRETTY DISTURBING.

FATHER: IT IS. AND THAT'S WHAT HAPPENS WHEN YOU DON'T HAVE GOD. AND YOU DON'T HAVE, YOU DON'T GROW UP WITH ANY, ANY RULES OR ANY ETHICS.

CHILD: I GREW UP WITH RULES AND ETHICS. I GREW UP WITH RULES AND ETHICS IMPOSED ON ME BY YOU ALL THE TIME. I'M NOT IN SUCH A GOOD PLACE NOW.

FATHER: WELL, THERE IS A BALANCE AND I DIDN'T HAVE, I, I... YOU HAD TOO MANY, I HAD TOO FEW. I DIDN'T HAVE ANY GUIDING SPIRIT. I NEVER THOUGHT WHEN I'D BE DOING STUFF THAT THERE WAS A GOD UP IN THE SKY, OR WHEREVER GOD IS, WHO IS WATCHING MY ACTIONS. AND, AND I DIDN'T HAVE ANY ACCOUNTABILITY TO ANYONE BUT MYSELF. AND I WAS VERY ETHICAL IN MY RULES, LIKE I, I HAD MY RULES. LIKE, I WOULDN'T CHEAT, YOU KNOW I WOULDN'T CHEAT ON MOM OR LIKE WHICH BASICALLY DID BUT I MEAN I WAS LIKE ALL THROUGH COLLEGE WOULDN'T CHEAT ON MOM. I HAD GIRLS WHO WERE INTERESTED I JUST WOULD TURN THEM AWAY ALL THROUGH, THROUGH LIFE.

CHILD: OK. MOM WAS LIKE THE HOTTEST GIRL YOU'RE EVER GONNA FIND. I MEAN

FATHER: WELL THAT WASN'T, THAT ISN'T HOW (A) THAT'S NOT HOW GUYS THINK AND (B) THAT'S NOT, THAT'S TRUE, BUT MOM WASN'T', ONE OF THE PROBLEMS IS THAT MOM IS NOT MY IDEAL, LIKE LOOKING WOMAN, FROM A BODY STANDPOINT, YOU WERE.

CHILD: BUT MOM IS GORGEOUS. IN COLLEGE AND IN HIGH SCHOOL SHE WAS PRETTIER THAN I'LL EVER BE.

FATHER: YEAH, BUT HER BODY WASN'T, HER BODY HAS ALWAYS BEEN

CHILD: OK. I SEE.

FATHER: AND, AND

CHILD: WHERE YOU ARE GOING WITH THAT

FATHER: AND SAY THAT PEOPLE'S, THEY SAY THAT PEOPLE'S UM, SOMETIMES YOUR DAUGHTER BECOMES LIKE THE PERFECT VERSION OF YOUR WIFE, PHYSICALLY, BUT BECAUSE THEY'RE YOUNGER AND EVERYTHING'S TIGHT AND LOOKS RIGHT AND THAT WAS YOU. YOU WERE, YOU WERE PHYSICALLY THE MORE, THE MOST BEAUTIFUL BODY THAT I HAVE, COULD'VE IMAGINED AND THAT WAS NOT, THAT WAS ANOTHER THING THAT WAS UNHEALTHY. SO ALL THESE THINGS ARE UNHEALTHY, THERE, THERE NO, I'M NOT TRYING TO DO EXCUSES. IT WAS TOTALLY EFF'D UP. I'M TOTALLY SORRY. I AM GOING TO GET TREATMENT.

CHILD: IF YOU'RE TOTALLY SORRY, AND YOU'RE SO REMORSEFUL, AND YOU THINK THAT EVERYTHING YOU DID WAS WRONG, WHY HAVE YOU HIRED THE TOP DOG ATTORNEY?

FATHER: BECAUSE I'M, I WANT YOU TO HAVE THE ABILITY TO CHOOSE MY, ANYTIME YOU GET, ANYTIME YOU GET INVESTIGATED YOU NEED TO GET A LAWYER.

CHILD: BUT YOU DON'T NEED TO GET A LAWYER THAT COSTS LIKE 25 GRAND AT THE START.

FATHER: HE COSTS 25 GRAND IF I GO TO TRIAL. AND THAT'S A RETAINER, IT'S NOT HOW MUCH IT COSTS. A RETAINER IS, YOU PAY THEM THE MONEY UP FRONT AND THEN THEY

CHILD: I ONLY HAVE 15 GRAND IN MY COLLEGE FUND.

FATHER: I HOPE I DON'T HAVE TO USE THAT, HON, AND I WON'T IF YOU DON'T WANT ME TO. I'VE, I'M, LET ME GET TO THAT BECAUSE I WANT TO ADDRESS THAT. YOU FEEL LIKE I FEEL THAT EVERYONE THINKS THAT I'M TRYING TO GET OUT OF THIS.

CHILD: EVERYONE DOES FEEL THAT YOU'RE TRYING TO GET OUT OF THIS. IT COMPLETELY LOOKS LIKE YOU ARE. YOU'VE HIRED THE TOP ATTORNEY IN TOWN.

FATHER: I HIRED, I CALLED EIGHT, LIKE TEN LAWYERS AND NO ONE WOULD TAKE ME BECAUSE THEY ALL DO CONTRACT LAW. AND THEN I WAS FINALLY TOLD THAT THIS GUY, AND I JUST STUMBLED INTO HIS OFFICE.

CHILD: I, HONESTLY DON'T REALLY BELIEVE THAT. YOU TEND TO DO A LOT OF RESEARCH ON STUFF. YOU KNOW WHAT'S GOING ON.

FATHER: NO

CHILD: YOU ARE A PENNY PINCHER. AND YOU JUST STUMBLED INTO A TOP LAWYER'S OFFICE AND YOU ARE LIKE, "OH, THE LAST ONE, I BETTER I BETTER COUGH UP"

FATHER: THE ONLY ONE, I CALLED THE ONES, THE ONE FROM CHURCH, I HAD A FRIEND CALL THE ONE FROM CHURCH TO ASK IF ANY OF THEM WOULD TAKE ME. NONE OF THEM WOULD TAKE ME, SO I JUST STARTED GOING DOWN THROUGH THE PHONE BOOK. AND, AND I DIDN'T GO TO HIM BECAUSE HE DIDN'T HAVE AN AD. AND THEN THE PERSON I TALKED TO, FINALLY THE ONLY ONE WHO GOT BACK TO ME SAID, "IF IT'S CRIMINAL, YOU SHOULD CALL THIS GUY." I'M NOT LYING. I'M TELLING YOU, I MEAN, I'M NOT LYING. SO THEN I GO INTO THE TOP ATTORNEY'S OFFICE AND HE SAYS, "YOU'RE IN BIG TROUBLE. YOU NEED TO DO THIS, THIS, AND THIS." AND, SO I DID. AND THEN

CHILD: WHY DO YOU CARE HOW BIG OF TROUBLE YOU'RE IN IS MY POINT. BECAUSE

FATHER: I'M GETTING THERE. YOU ARE THE ONE WHO WAS HURT. MOM

CHILD: I AM NOT THE ONLY ONE WHO WAS HURT. YOU CAN'T THINK LIKE THAT. YOUR ACTIONS HAVE HURT SO MANY PEOPLE, DAD.

FATHER: YOU ARE THE ONE

CHILD: I'M NOT TRYING TO BE MEAN OR

FATHER: I'M NOT TRYING TO SAY, I'M NOT TRYING TO SAY THAT I DIDN'T HURT OTHER PEOPLE, AND THAT MOM ISN'T HURT BY ALL OF THIS. I DON'T BELIEVE THAT.

CHILD: BUT YOU DO REALIZE THAT EVEN IF LIKE NOTHING HAPPENED, EVEN IF THERE WAS NO LEGAL REPERCUSSIONS, THAT MOM WOULD NEVER, YOUR MARRIAGE WOULD NEVER REUNITE. AND THAT MOM WOULD GET SOME KIND OF RESTRAINING ORDER AGAINST YOU. YOU DO REALIZE THAT AFTER EVERYTHING YOU HAVE DONE, SHE DOES NOT WANT YOU IN OUR LIVES. AND SO YOU'RE NOT GOING TO BE IN OUR LIVES. SHE IS JUST NOT GOING TO ALLOW IT TO HAPPEN.

FATHER: I DON'T BELIEVE THAT.

CHILD: WHY DO YOU NOT BELIEVE THAT?

FATHER: CAUSE I'M NOT, I'M NOT A THREAT ANYMORE. I'M CHANGED. SHE'S SEEN TWO YEARS OF ME CHANGED.

CHILD: OK. SO CONTINUE.

FATHER: ALL ALONG I HAVE SAID TO YOU THAT WHATEVER YOU, HOWEVER YOU WANT THIS TO PLAY OUT, THAT'S UP TO YOU. MOM STARTED INCLUDING A LOT OF PEOPLE IN THIS. AND, AND TR, AND SH, AND HER PARENTS. AND I WAS UNCOMFORTABLE. THEY WERE DRIVING, THEY WERE DRIVING HOW THIS PLAYED OUT, AND NOT YOU. AND THAT THEY WERE DRIVING, THEY WERE GONNA DRIVE THE PUNISHMENT, NOT YOU. ACTUALLY THEY WOULD LOSE CONTROL OF PUNISHMENT. THE POLICE WOULD TAKE CONTROL OF PUNISHMENT. CAUSE THE POLICE DON'T CARE WHAT YOU WANT OR WHAT MOM WANTS. THEIR JOB IS TO PROSECUTE SOMEONE WHO COMMITS A CRIME.

CHILD: THE POLICE CARE IF SOMEONE WHO IS A REGISTERED SEX OFFENDER IS A REGISTERED SEX OFFENDER. SO THAT THEY CANNOT CONTINUE TO OFFEND.

FATHER: NO. THEY DO CARE ABOUT THAT, BUT THEY ALSO, THEY WANT THE, THEY WANT TO PUT AWAY THE CRIMINAL. AND THEY DON'T CARE IF

CHILD: DO YOU CONSIDER YOURSELF A CRIMINAL?

FATHER: YEAH

CHILD: SO, WHY DO YOU FEEL YOU SHOULD BE EXEMPTED FROM THE NORMAL PROCEDURES?

FATHER: I'M NOT EXEMPTED FROM THE NORMAL PROCEDURES. I'M

CHILD: ALL RIGHT, CONTINUE

FATHER: NOT SURE WHAT YOU'RE SAYING

CHILD: WELL, YOU SEEM TO BE SAYING THAT POLICE WANT TO PUT AWAY CRIMINALS. POLICE WANT TO GET RID OF BAD GUYS AND THEY JUST DON'T

FATHER: RIGHT. THE POLICE WANT TO DO, UM, THE POLICE DON'T CARE WHAT THE VICTIM WANTS. THEY HAVE THEIR OWN SET OF... THEIR OWN AGENDA.

CHILD: BASICALLY, YOU'RE PUTTING ALL THE PRESSURE ON ME TO DECIDE IF I THINK YOU SHOULD GO TO JAIL OR NOT.

FATHER: I THINK THAT'S THE RIGHT THING. IT'S NOT THAT I'M TRYING TO PUT PRESSURE ON YOU, I THINK IF YOU DON'T, IF YOU WANT ME TO BE ABLE TO SUPPORT YOU FINANCIALLY AND DON'T WANT ME IN JAIL, THEN THAT SHOULD BE YOUR RIGHT AND IF YOU WANT ME TO HAVE NOTHING TO DO WITH THE FAMILY THAT SHOULD BE YOUR RIGHT. I DON'T.

CHILD: DO YOU NOT UNDERSTAND HOW UNHEALTHY IT IS TO PUT THAT PRESSURE ON A TEENAGE GIRL? TO PUT THAT PRESSURE ON YOUR DAUGHTER? I MEAN THAT'S

FATHER: IT'S NOT, IT'S THIS, PRESSURE IS NOT, YEAH, BUT DO YOU UM, REALIZE HOW UM, HOW WELL, IN MY MIND I FEEL IT'S ALSO SUPER UNHEALTHY IF YOU DIDN'T WANT ME TO GO TO JAIL FOR 20 YEARS AND THE POLICE TOLD ME, THE POLICE DECIDED THAT BASED ON ALL THEIR EVIDENCE THAT THAT'S WHAT WAS GOING TO HAPPEN. AND THEN YOU, AND YOU SAY, "WELL THAT'S NOT WHAT I WANTED TO HAPPEN." AND THEN YOU WOULD HAVE THE GUILT OF ME BEING IN JAIL FOR 20 YEARS

CHILD: AND WHAT IF I DON'T KNOW WHAT SHOULD HAPPEN? THAT I THINK MAYBE YOU SHOULD GO TO JAIL AND THEN I'VE GOT THE GUILT THAT I'VE SENT MY FATHER TO JAIL. YOU ARE JUST

FATHER: LOWER YOUR VOICE.

CHILD: YOU ARE COMPLETELY MESSING WITH MY HEAD RIGHT NOW. AND I THINK

FATHER: I'M NOT TRYING TO HONEY, I'M TRYING TO EMPOWER YOU. I'M TRYING TO

CHILD: OK

FATHER: I'M TRYING TO SAY, WHAT I'M TRYING TO PROTECT IS NOT ME. WHAT I'M TRYING TO PROTECT IS YOU.

CHILD: OK. . .

FATHER: I AM NOT DOING STUFF TO HURT THE FAMILY. I AM DOING STUFF TO TRY TO HELP THE FAMILY. AND I HAVE BEEN ALL ALONG. AND I HAVE A PROBLEM AND I SCREWED UP YOU AND I SCREWED UP THE FAMILY CAUSE OF THIS PROBLEM. BUT IT DOESN'T MEAN THAT EVERYTHING I'VE BEEN DOING IS FAKE OR BAD. THAT'S JUST NOT TRUE.

CHILD: OK

FATHER: AND THE TOP DOG ATTORNEY OR WHATEVER, I'VE SEEN HIM FOR LIKE AN HOUR. I'M EXTREMELY CAUTIOUS ABOUT HOW MUCH I'VE SEEN HIM...UNLIKE MOM THAT TALKS TO LAWYERS LEFT AND RIGHT. I HAVEN'T ... I'VE TOLD HIM I DON'T WANT TO PAY A LOT OF MONEY AND SO I'M ONLY GOING TO CALL HIM WHEN IT'S IMPORTANT. AND I'VE SEEN HIM FOR LIKE AN HOUR. AND I DON'T CALL HIM ON THE PHONE, AND I DON'T GO VISIT HIM. I'M LIKE SUPER CAUTIOUS ABOUT USING HIM BECAUSE OF HOW MUCH HE COSTS.

FATHER: AND I TOLD MOM IF SHE WANTS TO GET A...A YOU KNOW, FINANCIAL AGREEMENT AND ME NOT BEING ABLE TO SEE KIDS AND ALL THAT KIND OF STUFF THEN DON'T MAKE IT A COURT BATTLE. BECAUSE I DON'T WANT US TO WASTE THE MONEY WE DON'T HAVE. I TOLD HER JUST INCLUDE ME AND I'LL WORK WITH YOU AND WE'LL GET IT DONE. I'M NOT TRYING TO HURT THE FAMILY FINANCIALLY.

CHILD: OH. OK. SO I WANT TO ASK YOU MORE ABOUT THINGS THAT YOU REMEMBER.

FATHER: OK

CHILD: DO YOU REMEMBER COMING INTO MY ROOM IN THE MORNINGS AND GETTING IN BED WITH ME?

FATHER: NO

CHILD: BECAUSE I REMEMBER THAT

FATHER: I DON'T. ACTUALLY GETTING INTO BED WITH YOU?

CHILD: GETTING INTO BED WITH ME.

FATHER: SITTING ON YOUR BED OR....?

CHILD: GETTING INTO BED WITH ME.

FATHER: IN THE MORNING?

CHILD: YES

FATHER: I DON'T WANT TO DENY WHAT YOU SAID. JUST DON'T REMEMBER DOING THAT. I DID. OH, DID I JUST HUG YOU?

CHILD: I DON'T THINK SO.

FATHER: WHEN I WOULD COME HOME FROM DRINKING I WOULD GET INTO BED WITH YOU. I DON'T REMEMBER DOING THAT IN THE MORNING.

CHILD: I HAVE SKEWED PERCEPTIONS OF TIME BECAUSE I WAS HOMESCHOOLED.

FATHER: I DON'T BELIEVE I WOULD GET INTO BED WITH YOU IN THE MORNING CAUSE THAT JUST WASN'T WHAT I WOULD DO. IN THE MORNING IF I WAS GOING TO DO SOMETHING, I'D COME INTO YOUR ROOM AND MASTURBATE. AND I WOULD LOOK AT YOU AND I MIGHT TRY TO LIFT UP YOUR SHIRT. I MIGHT TRY TO TOUCH YOUR STOMACH. BUT THAT WAS VERY RARE. LIKE MOST OF THE TIMES IT WAS JUST LIKE UM, HAD

CHILD: WHAT ABOUT TOUCHING MY BREASTS?

FATHER: I HAD THREE MINUTES ON THE WAY TO WORK, SO I WOULD JUST MASTURBATE AND GO IN THE SHOWER AND MASTURBATE AND THAT WAS IT.

CHILD: THAT, WHAT ABOUT TOUCHING MY BREASTS?

FATHER: I WAS INTERESTED IN IT. I REMEMBER PICKING YOU UP WHEN YOU WERE SLEEPING ONCE AND PUTTING MY HAND ON YOUR BREAST AS I WAS CARRYING YOU BECAUSE I WANTED TO FEEL YOUR BREAST AND I WAS INTERESTED IN THEM SO IF I DID TOUCH THEM, I DON'T REMEMBER TOUCHING YOUR BREASTS EXCEPT FOR THAT TIME WITH PICKING YOU UP AND HOLDING AND HAVING MY HAND ON YOUR BREAST. BUT I KNOW THAT I WAS INTERESTED SO IF UM, AGAIN, IT WOULDN'T SURPRISE ME THAT I, IF YOU REMEMBER IT, IT'S TRUE. IF YOU DON'T REMEMBER IT, IT STILL COULD BE TRUE. I DON'T REMEMBER ACTUALLY TOUCHING YOUR BREASTS BUT THERE IS NOTHING ABOUT MY PATTERNS THAT WOULD MAKE ME THINK I WOULDN'T DO THAT.

CHILD: OK. UM, WHAT ABOUT WHEN YOU WOULD GET IN BED WITH ME AT NIGHT.

FATHER: IF I WAS DRINKING AND I'D GET INTO BED WITH YOU, I WOULD PUT MY HAND ON YOUR, AROUND YOUR STOMACH AND AND HUG YOU AND I WOULD HAVE IMPURE THOUGHTS. AND SO THEN, I DON'T KNOW. I DON'T KNOW IF I WOULD MASTURBATE OR IF I WOULD TRY TO TOUCH YOU OR

CHILD: WHAT DO YOU MEAN YOU DON'T KNOW?

FATHER: I DON'T KNOW WHAT I WOULD DO. I DON'T. I DON'T.

CHILD: YOU JUST DON'T REMEMBER ?

FATHER: I DON'T KNOW IF I WOULD MASTURBATE. I DON'T THINK I WOULD MASTURBATE TO THE POINT OF ORGASM BECAUSE I WOULD ACTUALLY BE THINKING I WAS GOING TO GO INTO BED AND WITH MOM AND HAVE SEX OR BE SEXUAL WITH HER...IT WAS ALMOST JUST LIKE

CHILD: WOULD YOU HAVE MASTURBATED WHILE TOUCHING ME?

FATHER: COULD HAVE.

CHILD: OK

FATHER: I'M SURE WHEN I PUT MY HAND ON YOUR, IN THE MORNING WHEN I PUT MY HAND ON YOUR STOMACH I WOULD MASTURBATE AT THAT TIME. BECAUSE THAT WOULD BE WHY I WOULD DO IT.

CHILD: DO YOU EVER GET... YOU ONLY PUT YOUR HAND ON MY STOMACH?

FATHER: NO. IF, AND THEN IF I PUT MY HAND LOWER, WOULD I, YOU KNOW THE SAME THING WE WERE TALKING ABOUT EARLIER.

CHILD: I REMEMBER THINGS LIKE THIS HAPPENING WITH THE FREQUENCY ON AVERAGE, LET'S SAY IN ALL THE YEARS THAT IT OCCURRED, OF ABOUT TWICE A MONTH.

FATHER: I THINK

CHILD: DO YOU THINK THAT FREQUENCY IS

FATHER: I THINK THE FREQUENCY OF

CHILD: POSSIBLE?

FATHER: ME MASTURBATING IN YOUR ROOM WAS HIGHER THAN TWICE A MONTH.

CHILD: YEAH. NO. I'M SURE IT WAS BUT I'M TELLING YOU WHAT I REMEMBER.

FATHER: I THINK OF YOU BEING TOUCHED I WOULD THINK, I WOULD THINK, I WOULD NOT THINK IT'S ANYWHERE NEAR THAT IF WE WERE JUST

TALKING ABOUT MORNING CAUSE THAT WAS LIKE A THRESHOLD I REALLY WOULDN'T CROSS. AND I DON'T REMEMBER. LIKE THERE WAS TOUCHING YOU WAS PRETTY MUCH OFF LIMITS. I'D GET NEAR YOU, LIKE CLOSE. LIKE A FEW FEET AWAY FROM YOU AS YOU ARE IN YOUR BED BUT WOULD REALLY, TOUCH YOU WAS REALLY, REALLY, VERY OFF LIMITS SO I'M, I'M..

CHILD: I [CRYING] I DON'T THINK I BELIEVE THAT UH BECAUSE

FATHER: OFF LIMITS. THAT'S MY, I'M JUST TELLING YOU MY MEMORY HON

CHILD: OK

FATHER: I DON'T DISAGREE WITH WHAT YOU'RE SAYING. IT COULD HAVE BEEN THAT OFTEN, BUT I BELIEVE, I BELIEVE THAT IF I WERE TOUCHING YOU THAT WAS AT NIGHT TIME AND IF I, IN THE MORNINGS THERE WASN'T TOUCHING GOING ON. GENERALLY, VERY, TO A LARGE DEGREE.

CHILD: WHY DO YOU THINK THAT THEY PUT SEX OFFENDERS IN JAIL?

FATHER: TO PUNISH THEM.

CHILD: WHY ELSE?

FATHER: TO PUNISH THEM. THEY DON'T PUT THEM IN JAIL TO REHABILITATE THEM. THEY DON'T PUT THEM IN JAIL TO KEEP THEM AWAY FROM OFFENDING.

CHILD: I'M PRETTY SURE THE GOAL IS TO KEEP THEM FROM OFFENDING.

FATHER: THEY CAN'T PUT THEM AWAY FOR LIFE THOUGH.

CHILD: THEY COULD PUT THEM AWAY FOR LIFE.

FATHER: THEY DON'T. THEY NEVER DO.

CHILD: YOU KNOW WHAT THE SENTENCES ARE.

FATHER: I DO. BUT THEY NEVER DO. THEY'RE NOT GOING TO PUT ME AWAY FOR LIFE. EVEN, IF, EVEN, NO MATTER WHAT. I MEAN IF YOU SAID I TOUCHED YOU A HUNDRED TIMES, THEY'RE NOT GOING OT PUT ME AWAY FOR LIFE. THEY JUST DON'T DO THAT.

CHILD: [SIGHS]

FATHER: SO, I'M GONNA BE OUT EVENTUALLY. I HAVEN'T DONE ANYTHING FOR OVER THREE YEARS.

CHILD: BUT YOU'VE KEPT LYING. IN THESE TWO YEARS YOU'VE SAID, "I'M A CHANGED MAN. YOU'VE SEEN THAT. FOR TWO YEARS I'VE BEEN A CHANGED MAN." YOU'VE STILL BEEN LYING ABOUT THINGS. YOU'VE STILL NOT BEEN FORTHCOMING, YOU'VE STILL BEEN EXTREMELY MANIPULATIVE [TALKING OVER HER FATHER] DO YOU AGREE WITH ALL THAT? YOU'VE STILL BEEN EXTREMELY MANIPULATIVE, AND NOT FORTHCOMING, AND LYING. IN THOSE TWO YEARS YOU SAY YOU'VE BEEN A CHANGED MAN.

FATHER: I'VE BEEN TRYING TO PROTECT PEOPLE. I'VE BEEN TRYING... LET ME ASK YOU IF, SAY UM, THROW OUT HERE, OK WELL, NONE OF THESE THINGS ARE GOING TO SOUND GOOD BUT, SAY I, UM, SAY I WHEN YOU WERE THREE THAT I HAD DONE SOMETHING HORRIBLE TO YOU. DIDN'T HAPPEN. I NEVER DID ANYTHING WHEN YOU WERE THREE. SHOULD I SAY THAT UM WHEN YOU WERE 12 THAT I STARTED UH THAT I DID SOMETHING, WAS CAUGHT. NOW SHOULD I BRING UP THE FACT THAT WHEN YOU WERE THREE I DID SOMETHING? OR IS THAT GOING TO JUST SCREW YOU UP MORE? LIKE THE MASTURBATING.

CHILD: YOU SHOULD BE HONEST.

FATHER: THE MASTURBATING STUFF, I DIDN'T KNOW IF YOU KNEW THAT AND I DIDN'T WANT TO LIKE FURTHER CONFUSE YOU AND TO MAKE YOU

CHILD: PROBABLY SHOULD HAVE AVOIDED THE SITUATION IN THE FIRST PLACE.

FATHER: I KNOW BUT...

CHILD: BUT THEN YOU SHOULD HAVE BEEN HONEST. YOU DIDN'T TELL MOM FOR SUCH A LONG TIME. YOU COULD HAVE BEEN HONEST WITH A GREAT NUMBER OF PEOPLE.

FATHER: I WAS SO HONEST [TALKING OVER CHILD] WITH MOM. WHEN I WAS HONEST SHE LEFT ME AND KICKED ME OUT OF THE HOUSE THE NEXT DAY. THAT'S FINE I WANTED TO HAVE A CHANCE TO MAKE THINGS RIGHT.

CHILD: BUT YOU CAN'T MAKE THINGS RIGHT WITHOUT BEING HONEST. IF SHE WANTS TO HAVE THAT REACTION TO YOUR HONESTY, SHE'S TOTALLY ALLOWED TO.

FATHER: SHE, I WASN'T HURTING ANYONE FOR THOSE, THOSE EXTRA TWO YEARS I GOT. I WASN'T HURTING ANYONE AND I WAS TRYING TO REPAIR ALL THE BROKENNESS.

CHILD: DAD! YOU DID A GREAT JOB IN THOSE TWO YEARS EXCEPT FOR...

FATHER: GONNA GET HONEST. I WAS JUST TRYING TO DO AS MUCH REPAIR AS I COULD SO I WAS, SO EVERYONE WAS AS STRONG AS THEY COULD DEAL WITH IT, IF IT WAS GONNA COME OUT. I WASN'T, I WASN'T THINKING I WAS GONNA GET AWAY WITH STUFF FOREVER, I ALWAYS WANTED TO TELL MOM BUT I JUST WANTED TO GET SOME HEALING IN FIRST, THEN I WAS TRYING TO GET THAT WITH YOU. I WAS TRYING TO GET IT WITH MOM.

CHILD: ALL RIGHT. SO LET'S CUT TO THE CHASE THEN. SO IS THE BASIC PART OF THIS DISCUSSION THAT YOU WANT ME TO KNOW THAT I AM RESPONSIBLE FOR YOUR LEGAL OUTCOME IN THIS SITUATION?

FATHER: NO. THE POINT OF THIS CONVERSATION IS THAT YOU ... YOU ARE 100% UM RIGHT. EVERYTHING YOU THINK HAPPENED HAPPENED. AND I'M SORRY. AND I AM WILLING TO HAVE THIS GO HOWEVER YOU WANT IT TO. AND IF WHAT YOU WANT TO HAVE HAPPEN IS THAT YOU DON'T HAVE ANY CONTROL OVER IT, YOU WANT TO PASS THAT ON, I GUESS THAT'S FINE. I, I FELT THAT IT WAS IMPORTANT THAT IF YOU WANTED ME, I DIDN'T THINK THAT YOU WANTED ANY OF THIS TO HAPPEN. I THOUGHT THAT THIS WAS BEING DRIVEN BY A FRIEND OF MOM'S AND MOM. AND SO I DIDN'T WANT TO GO, BE LIKE GOING DOWN SOME AVENUE AND YOU JUST BEING PULLED ALONG AND LIKE, BEING "LIKE WAIT A SEC, THAT'S NOT WHAT I WANTED TO HAPPEN." I JUST DIDN'T WANT THAT TO HAPPEN, AND SO

CHILD: OK. I APPRECIATE THE THOUGHT. I WOULDN'T, I WOULDN'T LET THAT HAPPEN. I'M TOO STRONG WILLED TO LET THAT HAPPEN. I KEPT THIS A SECRET FOR AN UNGODLY AMOUNT OF TIME BECAUSE I DIDN'T WANT THAT TO HAPPEN, AND THEN I DECIDED THAT IT WAS TIME TO BE TRUTHFUL WITH PEOPLE. AND THE BEST WAY TO GET HEALING FOR MYSELF WAS TO BE TRUTHFUL. AND I THINK THAT'S THE BEST WAY FOR EVERYONE TO GET HEALING.

FATHER: I DO TOO. AND I'M GOING TO BE TRUTHFUL WITH MY TREATMENT. IN MY TREATMENT THAT I DO AND...

CHILD: BETTER BEING TRUTHFUL ABOUT ALL YOUR STUFF.

FATHER: I JUST UM. I DON'T WANT THIS TO BE MORE OF A BURDEN ON YOU. SO THAT'S NOT WHAT I WANT. I DON'T WANT TO SAY THIS IS UP TO YOU. BUT I WILL SAY THAT IF YOU DON'T WANT ME TO CONTEST ANYTHING, THEN I WILL JUST HAVE MY LAWYER GET... "LET'S NEGOTIATE." YOU KNOW, YOU KNOW, IN AGREEMENT WITH THE POLICE ON HOW I WANT TO GO TO JAIL AND THAT STUFF.

CHILD: SO, PLEADING GUILTY THEN?

FATHER: YEAH, IF THAT'S WHAT YOU WANT, THAT'S WHAT I'LL DO.

CHILD: I DON'T, I'M NOT GOING TO SAY LIKE I WANT YOU TO GO TO JAIL. I, DON'T KNOW WHAT I WANT. SO I'M JUST GOING TO TURN IT OVER TO SOMEONE ELSE.

FATHER: WELL, YOU ARE TOO STRONG TO DO THAT. I TRUST YOU MORE THAN ANYONE. IT'S NOT THAT I THINK THAT YOU ARE MORE LIKELY TO LET ME OFF, BUT NO MATTER WHAT YOU SAY YOU ARE THE ONE, YOU ARE THE VICTIM HERE. MOM IS THE VICTIM OF A CRAPPY HUSBAND. SHE IS NOT THE VICTIM OF SEXUAL ABUSE. SHE CAN DIVORCE ME. THAT'S HER RIGHT. IF YOU HAVE A CRAPPY HUSBAND IT'S A DIVORCE THEN. IT'S NOT TO SEND THEM TO JAIL.

CHILD: BUT AN INCESTUAL HUSBAND CAN BE SENT TO JAIL.

FATHER: BECAUSE OF WHAT I DID WITH YOU, NOT BECAUSE OF WHAT I DID WITH OR TO HER.

CHILD: YES.

FATHER: I'M SAYING SHE DID NOT HAVE, SHE WAS NOT THE VICTIM OF THE CRIME THAT I WOULD BE GOING TO JAIL FOR WITH YOU. THIS SHOULD BE YOUR CALL.

CHILD: WHAT IF I WAS LIKE: "OK. YEAH, GIVE HIM THE MAXIMUM SENTENCE."

FATHER: THEN THAT'S WHAT I'LL TELL THE GUY

CHILD: AND THEN YOU WOULD HATE ME FOREVER?

FATHER: NO. I'LL LOVE YOU FOREVER...

CHILD: BECAUSE I DON'T KNOW YET HOW I'M GOING TO DECIDE FOR THIS TO PLAY OUT.

FATHER: I DON'T HAVE ANY ILL WILL FOR YOU AND NEVER WOULD I.

CHILD: OK

FATHER: I DON'T. YOU KNOW ME GOING TO JAIL IS THE RIGHT, IS I DON'T KNOW IF IT IS BEST FOR THE FAMILY? BUT IT CERTAINLY A PROPER PUNISHMENT, SO I'M NOT GOING TO COMPLAIN ABOUT A PROPER PUNISHMENT.

CHILD: AND YOU BEING AWAY FROM THE FAMILY IS SOMETHING THAT SHOULD HAPPEN. FOR SOME TIME, BECAUSE

FATHER: THEN, I'M GOING TO DO A YEAR IN TREATMENT. I'M GOING TO BE AWAY FROM THE FAMILY FOR A YEAR.

CHILD: HOW IS THAT BEING FINANCED?

FATHER: I'M DOING THE ONE THAT IS, ON UM, THAT I CAN DO WHILE I WORK. BUT I CAN'T BE AROUND THE FAMILY CAUSE I NEED TO FOCUS ON IT. IT'S LIKE A, THEY TAKE THE 45 DAY ONE THEY EXPAND IT TO A YEAR SO THAT YOU CAN WORK.

CHILD: DAD, MY FRIEND IS WAITING FOR ME. I HONESTLY HAVE TO GO MEET HER.

FATHER: HERE IS A LETTER.

CHILD: THANK YOU.

FATHER: IT'S GOING TO BE PRETTY CHRISTIAN, SO IF YOU'RE NOT CHRISTIAN DON'T THINK I'M CRAZY. IT'S WHAT I BELIEVE. AND I HOPE THAT YOU WILL BELIEVE IT AGAIN.

CHILD: OK

FATHER: I HAVEN'T DONE ANYTHING BESIDES WHAT YOU KNOW THAT I'VE DONE TO YOU.

CHILD: ALL RIGHT. THANK YOU. BYE.

After a grueling 49-minute conversation where Cal tries to explain away his bad decisions, offer empty apologies, and tell his daughter that his punishment should be decided by her, Clara watches as police apprehend her father, handcuffing him and escorting him to a vehicle where he was taken to jail. As the detectives and police were outside the building, incredulous at the conversation they just recorded, one of the officers said, out loud, "This guy cannot be around children."

Back at the Police Department, seated in a back room around a large table, I waited for my daughter to return. An officer walked in and stood at the front of the table. He was dressed in uniform as he made the following statement:

"Mrs. Bering," he said, "Cal Bering has been arrested and lodged at the Correctional Facility. I know this is difficult news for you and your family. Please let me know if there is anything that I can do for you."

"Can I have a hug?" I asked him.

With his bullet proof vest and all his gear on, the officer stood there and hugged me.

Shortly thereafter, Clara arrived and I helped her remove the tape holding the recording device to her stomach. Clara had to debrief with the detectives and I excused myself to go to the ladies' room and cry on the bathroom floor. A female officer interrupted my experience with the grey tile flooring. "Mrs. Bering, we will need you to make sure that you follow up on a few items. Please come back to the table when you are finished in here."

As if I were flossing my teeth in the ladies' room, the officer notified me and stepped out of the bathroom. I got up off of the cold tile flooring, which for some reason was incredibly grounding and comforting, and I walked back into the conference room, seating myself next to Clara who was really worn down.

When it was finally over, Clara and I left the precinct and headed outdoors, for the beach and the ocean.

"Well, there he goes for 25 years," uttered Clara. We were silent for the rest of the drive to the ocean. Neither one of us knew what had just happened. We both believed that Cal had a problem and at the same time, we believed he loved his family. Clara and I trusted that Cal would honor his word and take his punishment like he said he would.

Cal went to jail on Holy Thursday, 2011. That Good Friday felt as disorienting as a major earthquake. But, on Sunday, the sun came out, and the children and I headed off to the outdoor sunrise Easter service. I stood by my friend as her husband led the service in front of the glacier.

In a strange way, nothing had changed. I was still me—maybe more me than I'd been in a long time. The circumstances of my life had changed, and I knew intense challenges lay in store for us. But those paled in contrast to the relief I felt in that moment. My husband's mind-bending control over me—and my attempts to bend my own mind to accept his truth—had finally ceased. *This* was God's plan for us, the miracle in funny packaging. Our Resurrection Day.

3

A New Normal

You will be like a well-watered garden—
a spring whose water never fails.

Joel 2:25

I will restore the years
that the locusts have eaten.

Isaiah 58:11

I was now a lone bird, leading some very wounded fledglings. But, in my aloneness, I also felt newness. The incredible oppression in our home had shifted.

I had trouble wrapping my head around anything for too long, as events unfolded at light speed. It was terrifying. Here I was with young, angry, hurt, traumatized children, a beloved yellow Labrador Retriever, a mortgage on a five-bedroom house, car insurance bills, electric bills, cell phone bills, water and sewer bills, unpaid medical bills and no health insurance, and attorney's fees and other costs of civil and criminal trials— and I hadn't worked outside the home in over 15 years.

Overnight, the responsibility of providing for my children's emotional and material needs rested on me alone. While mourning the loss of all hope that my husband would become the man we needed—a hope that had strangely sustained me for most of my adult life—I also had to let go of the life that had enabled me to be home, nurturing and loving my children.

The loss of "our family," as I had thought of it for so long, and the loneliness that ensued, was almost unbearable, as grief overwhelmed and infiltrated all corners of my life. In my trauma, I did not know how to frame my pain for public consumption. The choice I made was to draw from two familiar and unshakeable forces that have always sustained and guided me: faith in God and running.

Immediately after he went to jail, Cal began harassing Clara and I with demands from attorneys. It was the beginning of an exhausting process of relentless legal battering in which I constantly defended myself, and my children.

At the request of Cal's divorce attorney, the judge ruled in favor of Cal's tactical motion for the involvement of a Guardian Ad Litem. A Guardian Ad Litem (GAL) is a person appointed by the court to advocate for the best interests of children. I fought the ruling because it made no sense to me—I did not need supervision. Clara's community of coaches, counselors and teachers were providing her with extra support and guidance. The judge denied my request and we ended up with a series of three GALs in our lives. Cal was legally allowed to assert control over us from his prison cell, as I was picking up the pieces of his destruction.

When Cal was put in jail in April of 2011 his mother, Joan, threatened to sue me within the first week for visitation with Andrew and Jason. I demanded privacy for my family, while the children adjusted to losing their father and I mourned the loss of my husband. Joan didn't take too well to that imperative. She bypassed my authority and directly contacted Clara through Facebook. Clara felt frightened and intimidated, so she blocked her from social media. Joan then alienated Clara as punishment because she didn't comply to her manipulation. Her sense of entitlement was strong and her anger was fierce when I denied her visitation with Andrew and Jason.

Joan attempted another avenue for visitation by befriending Nilly, the first GAL. Nilly told my first attorney that Joan had offered to support us but that I had turned her down. When she said this to my attorney, he fell back in his chair in a fit of laughter and when he came back to his senses, he said, "I'd like to see that in writing." He also said, "She is welcome to offer her financial assistance to her grandchildren at any time." The subject never came up again.

Joan usurped the financial abuse, holding her son's place for him while he was incarcerated. Her interest in my private financial affairs did not go unnoticed. As was brought to my attention by an incensed bank manager, a woman in her early 30's, whom I met with to discuss my accounts. She said that Cal's mother had been at the bank trying to get information about my accounts. I'm not sure what the exchange was that took place, but I'm certain it was unpleasant.

The manager exclaimed, "That woman is a pariah and a vampire! I called all of our branches and told them not to work with her and to report if she came in fishing for information."

Joan protected her abusive son. She personally funded his high-priced legal defense team, well-paid private investigators included, with the goal of discrediting my 15-year-old daughter. When given the opportunity, she quickly posted the $500,000 bail to temporarily release him from prison.

Later, in divorce proceedings, Cal would explain to the judge that he was financially strapped because his four siblings would not accept that any of their inheritance would be used for his legal defense. He informed the judge that he was repaying the debt to his mother in the amount of $1,000 per month. Cal prioritized his private loan over child support payments.

Joan periodically arrived in Alaska to navigate Cal's legal

circumstances. On one of her early visits, while my children and I were still vulnerable, I didn't want us to be victims of her endless schemes. To avoid an accidental encounter while she was in town, I took the kids and dog out to the new cabin on at the beach. I kept their normal school routines during the day, and we spent our late afternoons playing by the water on the embankment right outside the cabin. They did their homework by candle and flashlight in the evenings, enjoying three overnights of family time. Each morning we ate breakfast at the Waffle House before I dropped everyone at school.

It felt illicit, because I had been warned by the GAL not to go out of cell phone range due to the active legal proceedings. I deduced that state workers needed to conduct their business between 8am and 4pm. Taking the kids to the privacy of the cabin in the evening, out of cell phone range, wasn't going to impact their work. We were not the criminals, but our sense of freedom was impacted.

Cal and his mother were punishing us for turning him in by all means possible.

Running

The new snow squeaks under my Sauconys. The little yellow house with blue trim that shelters my children recedes as I ascend the hill, pass the historic houses, cross the street, climb a set of metal-grate stairs, cross another street, and run up another set of stairs.

"You should be home enjoying Thanksgiving with your family. It's too dangerous to be out running in the wind and snow." My friend's words echo in my ear as I climb a little higher, past the old houses with neat firewood stacks that line the narrowing road.

Warning signs about keeping dogs on leashes and being alert for bear activity, along with a map of the steep terrain, remind me that I'm mortal. The sensation of stepping onto the trail is a drug that draws all of me under its spell. The soft brown earth beneath my feet persists under a thin layer of snow then transitions into rock before becoming a root-veined path. Step. Step. Step. Silence accompanies the acceleration of my heartbeat as my strong legs ascend the steep trail. My lungs expand and contract with the cold mountain air, breathing new life into my blood cells.

Oh to get deep enough into the trail's heart to open my own. My mountain once again assures me everything is going to be ok. Tears never threaten its equilibrium. The earth's strength boldly rises through the tender soles of my feet, enters the thick bones of my legs, and warms my screaming chest.

Words no human heart is strong enough to hear or

understand arise in me. My voice starts as a whisper and opens up to this audience of trees, dirt, snow, and ice, with a roar.

Why? Why did you let this happen to my daughter? Why did you let Jason suffer so? What do you expect of me? How am I supposed to carry this? How could you let this happen? Why? Why? Why? The loss is too great, Lord. The kids have suffered too much! What am I supposed to do? What do you want from me? I'm so sorry, Clara. I'm so sorry guys. I'm so sorry. I'm so sorry. Mommy is so sorry.

I run past a waterfall and turn around the first bend. A treacherous river of ice inevitably runs under every beautiful thick blanket of new snow. My hands and feet map the territory for me, locating a root, a patch of brush, or a frozen rock to stabilize me so I can I press on.

Passing the first picnic shelter and bench—a rest spot overlooking the scenic town—I look through an opening in the trees that frames the quaint, lighted homes and tight-knit community below. Mr. Rogers' neighborhood. The tall office building my estranged husband once worked in. The house that now holds my children, its foggy lighted windows emitting a warm glow.

My eyes search for roots I can launch my next step off of. Once again, I need my hands and feet to feel my way around the patch of glass lurking under the white powder. Traversing another corner, as I pass the next bench, my mind's eye sees my father sitting there six months ago, on a sunny day, amid the lush, bright kelly-green devil's club and blueberry bushes that engulf the trail in summer. I flash back to how I felt that day—awed by his willingness to hike his 70-year-old body up this mountain. I smile at the memory of him muttering the name he'd given to our hike— "a forced march."

My water bottle is usually easy to keep full in Alaska. But today the little creeks that tumble across the trails have frozen.

Snow replaces the fresh streams. Sparkling crystals melt as I press my warm tongue against the clean, white, one-of-a-kind flakes gathered in my cupped palm.

A quick stop is all I need. I can sense my body cooling ever so slightly, the sweat droplets on my skin bringing a mild chill to the back of my neck near the hair at the base of my ponytail.

My heart endeavors to make itself heard, to release the pressure and pain that I carry for my babies. My heart is a deep bruise beating. It reaches out to God, calling for His recognition, healing, protection, and renewal for my children. Beyond this cold, snowy mountain and this Thanksgiving Day, my heart is calling for God to heal all children who have been or are being abused. Almighty bring healing to those afflicted with a diseased heart that allows them to sexually abuse children.

Nearing the shuttered lodge, I remind myself to watch for frosty wooden boards placed on the trail to help hikers, runners, and tourists avoid muddying their shoes in the summer months. Like the trail below, the winter paints these planks with frost and ice before hiding them under the snow. Today, I decide it is safest to stay in the frozen footprints on the sides of the boards.

Through the biting wind and blowing snow, a man appears, walking toward me. My gut tightens with fear. He's got trekking poles in both hands. Probably in his 6os, he smiles as the distance between us closes. I can't fathom why anyone else would be up here, in this weather, on Thanksgiving Day. I offer a half of a smile and run on.

The presence of another human temporarily severs my connection to the mountain. I struggle to tune myself back into my surroundings. The lodge comes into view behind the blowing snow. I have a decision to make: Do I turn around here or keep climbing?

In the warmer months, there are trails to follow. Today, the taut white surface of a hot-dried fitted sheet stretches out before me. Nevertheless, I decide to keep going, up to the tall marker that had been installed in the early 1900s, near a rocky overhang at the mountain's first false summit. The snow starts to get deeper. For the first time in the hundreds of times I've run this mountain, I can't see the trail. Remnants of fireweed and devil's club protruding from the snow here and there provide a little bit of much-needed texture. I turn to look back over where I've been. My own footprints are filling in quickly with wind-blown drifts.

As I approach the top, snow wedges itself into the space between my wool ankle socks and my skin. The blanket of white leads me to the foot of the cross, where I crumple into a ball, sobbing. My ears hear my broken voice ask God aloud, "How are you going to fix this? I wish you didn't give this burden to me, to my children. I don't want this mess. You have to show me the way. Please don't leave us like this. Don't let us fail. Don't let my children suffer any more. Heal our lives, Lord." The falling snow attempts to accumulate on me, but my body heat transforms it into water that runs down my back and seeps into the ground at the foot of the cross.

There is no one to get me off this mountain but me. I force myself to stand. I block off one side of my nose and blow, then clear the second nostril. Ah, that felt great. While I have been losing it at the base of the cross, the wind has been busy trying to erase evidence of my climb. Enough of my footprints have survived to lead me back. I slip in places, then begin to laugh out loud as I slide and jump my way down. I sober up when my leg gets stuck in snow up to my groin. Thankful not to have hyperextended anything, I pull myself out and keep going. The lodge soon comes into view.

My feet dial into the music of the mountain with each percussive step. My heart is breathing now—alive and full. My chest is wide open. I touch the branches extending over the trail heading down to the hidden boards. So much love radiates from the trees; they sing to me as I pass, sharing their powerful energy with me, to bring home to my family. Lower and lower I descend, savoring every sensation, as my muscles carry my refreshed spirit closer to home. I can't wait to carry this new aliveness into our household; to share my exhilarated spirit with my children.

Ouch! My tailbone hits the ice hard. My elation turns to shock as the carefree steps lead to a careless fall. It takes me a moment to tell if I can move, think. I look around and see my only option is to slide forward. The ice-covered trail with its glazed edges has left me nothing to grab onto. I accumulate snow in my crotch and under the soles of my sneakers to slow my slide, as I steer my body to a lone patch of gravel. Leaning against the trail's upper bank, I grab onto leftover roots and stabilize myself with a toe on a rock while I plot my next move.

The exposure and adrenaline from the fall start to do a number on my fine motor skills. My ardor is dampened; I'm ready to be home. Picking up the pace, I arrive back at the best part—the straightaway before the overlook. Speaking aloud, I seek the frozen trail's permission to brace my foot against the small icy berm that demarcates its town-side margin. "Alright? Alright?" I ask.

Ow! Down again! Even harder this time. It takes a moment to feel anything. Unsure of the damage, I sit still, inventorying my back. I see my spine light up like an x-ray at the impact of that crash and momentarily fear the ramifications of moving an injured spine. But not moving is not an option. The only one getting you off this mountain is you, I tell myself. I stretch my leg, feeling for a new foothold. Sliding a short distance on my wet butt, very thoughtfully I press my sneaker's thin rubber sole into a patch of gravel. Okay. I bend my knee to draw my body closer to my foot and extend the other leg to a patch of root-laced ground.

My lungs draw in a deep breath of fresh cold air. Back on my *feet I pass the bench and slowly make my way down the last part of the trail. Once on the road, I sprint home over the long bridge and through the town's uppermost streets. I'm careful now on the metal-grated stairs. Fatigue has dulled my reaction time. I run past my friends' homes and into our little house.*

Once inside, I pry off my shoes and peel my sopping wet socks off my feet. Jason is stretched out on the couch. I squeeze his toes and head upstairs to see if Andrew needs anything. He had woken up sick earlier, but now assures me he's ok.

The old pastel painted door has a hot shower waiting for me on the other side. I step inside and stretch my damp, smelly, purple polyester running shirt over my head. My stiff, cold hands are of little use as I wrestle out of my sports bra and thick running pants. I open the white shower faucet and rotate it to hot. The steaming water rinses off the cold, as well as the dried salt of sweat and tears. Home, I whisper, smiling. I reach for the bar of soap and begin to wash off. When I touch the base of my spine, a pain shoots through me. Reminded anew of the times I have fallen, I take a deep breath and accept that the bruises are going to take some time to heal.

Basic and Not-So-Basic Needs

We move through places every day
that would never have been
if not for those who came before us.

Mitch Albom
The Five People You Meet in Heaven

It was lonely and scary for all of us to have our old family structure evaporate overnight. Cal had carefully constructed each of our places in the family; many years had gone into creating our patterns, now all of them were shaken and broken. Yes, Cal's absence was a good thing, but it was also disorienting.

"Basic" is the best word I can think of to describe where I found myself after Cal went to prison. The burden we carried was omnipresent but unclear; a heaviness persisted, but it was difficult to sort out why. I perpetually questioned myself. How could I make things better for my children? How could I be more supportive of Cal? How could I defuse our conflict with their father? I looked to my family for support.

My sister Adele came out to Alaska in April of 2012 when the trial was scheduled to take place. She walked with me and was in the courtroom with me and my friends as the criminal attorney asked for more time and the trial got delayed for the first of what would become many delays. This is poignant because, through the use of expensive legal counsel, Cal used the court system to over-extend my and the children's support system. He succeeded.

The abuse that my children and I endured caused my family, my mother and father, an immense amount of emotional pain. It was so distressing for them that they had to distance themselves in order to offer sustained support. This was very painful for me because I did not understand the way that it was impacting them. I just sensed their absence and incorrectly interpreted it as indifference, when the reality was much more severe. They were both in counseling to help them cope with the violence that my ex-husband imparted on my children and me. My siblings sought advice and brought the impact of my experience to counselors as well.

In the time frame that my ex-husband went to jail and got out and harassed us non-stop, my best friend's husband was diagnosed and succumbed to a brain tumor. I was reading about widowhood and I discovered something about grief, which was a huge component of what my immediate and extended family was experiencing. Loss of any type creates grief, and the grieving frequently undergo the experience of family not supporting them, not being there for them in their time of need. This knowledge helped me stop blaming my family for not supporting me in my very difficult situation. The truth was multidimensional. They *were* supporting us in the best way they knew how; they were grieving, and the collateral damage that my ex-husband caused by his self-serving molestations was unquantifiable.

I was pressured by the attorneys, but it was never enforced by the judge, to take the kids to visit their father in jail. I didn't want them to see him like that. *I* didn't want to see him like that. My mind was still expecting my husband to come home from work at the end of the day. I had to remind myself that he was gone forever. That he couldn't be around children because he is a predator. These truths were not yet internalized. These truths were very challenging to absorb.

Eventually I would realize that I would never make peace with Cal—not before his arrest and not after. Maybe it's better stated and feels more true to say that I learned to love my ex-husband for who he really is; completely broken and very dangerous. I now knew that to love him meant to never have contact with him again. I want to forgive him because it frees me up to enjoy my beautiful children and my own life.

Along the lines of basic, the most basic way I could help our family's rebuilding process was to find work. I went to the Job Center like it was a job. I had the best support team there, helping me write cover letters and spruce up my resumé. The people who worked with me at the job center were another stage to my healing. I was reminded that people were kind and caring.

The first job I took was as a receptionist at a busy doctor's office. This job, and the subsequent employment opportunities that I took, pulled me away from being there for my kids. In the summer of 2012, following the instruction of mental health professionals, I moved us to a new home so we could have a fresh start. It was a two-bedroom rental near where Clara worked and went to school. There was a large basement that Clara and I were going to make into an apartment for her. We bought new furniture and with a lot of hard work and help from friends we moved in. This turned out not to be a perfect arrangement. Clara's basement apartment had mold issues, Andrew wanted his own space, Jason missed the backyard swing and zip-line. The dog didn't complain, but he did let himself out on frequent enough walks that he made a name for himself at the Humane Society.

I was able to walk to work and the kids were able to walk to school. This was a big change for all of us. It was very convenient and made single parenting much easier. It was still a major adjustment. The kids didn't have a parent to go home to and I was new at work with no seniority, so I had to put work first. I cried as I walked to work, leaving them behind with so much for them to take on by themselves now.

Andrew stepped up as big brother to Jason. Andrew was now ten years old. He had pleaded with me to let him finish 5th grade at his elementary school. I painfully had to say no. Andrew joined a local swim team. He practiced with the swim team after school for his entire 5th grade year. The pool was right next to his school, which was right next to our house.

He also told me, "Mom, when I grow up you won't have to work. I'm going to buy a house and you can just lay on the couch and eat chips."

He thought a moment longer.

"Well, I might get sick of you. So, I'll build you your own house."

Jason was in childcare after school. He did not like it. He wanted to be home. Jason found a lot of comfort resting on the family dog and playing video games. I think the video games were his way out.

Andrew stayed heavily involved in swimming, skiing, and guitar lessons and performances. He also wanted to see his brother thrive. Jason suffered from untreated trauma and the way this trauma presented itself mirrored severe depression.

Andrew once looked at me with tears in his eyes and said, "I just want my brother back."

I hired babysitters and after-school care. And in the summers, I put them in camps for the entire summer. From 2012 – 2017 I paid for summer camps with no help from Cal. I applied for scholarships for every camp, every summer. The scholarships would reduce the cost, but it was still a few thousand dollars a summer to cover camp fees and provide the boys with activities.

Andrew loved the involvement and camaraderie. Jason was struggling. Andrew would try to get Jason involved and Jason would fight him every step of the way.

For camps that were not overnight, or when Jason was not old enough to attend overnight camps, I would use my lunch hour to transport the kids places. At the time it seemed hectic but some of it I look back on fondly. It was a great community and my kids had unprecedented opportunities. They participated in sailing camp, community center camps and activities, bible camp, 4-H programs, robotics, and summer church camps. There was a lot of good mixed with a lot of responsibility. Andrew had an uncanny sense of responsibility for his brother, his sister and even for me.

Both Andrew and Jason had started out on ski team and in little league baseball. I tried to maintain everything that we had done as a two-parent family. Ski team was an outlet that remained for Andrew. Jason couldn't handle the structure, but he loved skiing on his own.

Andrew's coach, without any fanfare, noticed that it was a struggle to get both Andrew and Jason out the door. For the next several ski seasons he picked Andrew up for practice and races. Jason and I would follow later in the day. Andrew developed into an excellent skier. His equipment was subsidized through a generous and caring ski team dad, who Cal used to work with. It wasn't until Andrew started to really take an interest in running, his freshman year in high school, that he decided to stop racing. It was a big deal to say goodbye to the racing and the ski team family. Instead, Andrew cross-country skied with the alpine team during the winter and ran track in the spring.

Jason struggled. He didn't want to participate in sports. He wouldn't go to the pool. He resentfully participated in camps. He had a real struggle with social activity. He didn't want to play the piano and wouldn't practice, despite his very experienced teacher telling him that he had the aptitude to be one of her best students.

So while Andrew dove into every activity that was available to him, Jason avoided every activity he could. It would take time for Jason to find his niche.

Sentencing

*Witnessing this horror first hand as a close friend who
helped to notify authorities, I have been shocked at the lack
of rights the family of an accuser has, to even attempt to
move on if that accused person so chooses to keep finances
and legal matters on hold. It has been a painful struggle that
is far from over for this family.*

Stella
Winter of 2013

At his initial sentencing hearing, Cal walked into the crowded
courtroom and sat down next to his defense attorney. The
judge informed him that, although he could not admit the
Glass warrant transcript into evidence, he could consider it at
sentencing. At the words "Glass warrant," Cal fell into a violent
seizure. His head shot back and his neck distended, so it
looked almost like a horse's neck. Clara and I instinctively
cried out for someone to call for help. He looked dead. We
were both terrified.

Cal went to jail on April 21, 2011, marking the beginning of a
legal battle to provide for the safety and security of my children
that I am still fighting to this day. In December of 2012, as we
were approaching the sentencing hearing, we were notified
that the D.A. who had been on our case up to this point would

not be at the sentencing because of a family emergency. On December 16, 2012, one day before the hearing, I walked up to talk to the new D.A.. But before this important meeting, I sent the following email to our friends and family:

Hello Friends and Family Members,

I really hope that you are enjoying the Holiday Season. The boys and I are in a church skit this morning. Andrew is the Pope, Jason is a sheep. I will play the part of Giovanna. This should be a winner!

Cal's sentencing hearing is tomorrow. I am meeting with a new D.A. today, who will be sitting in for the D.A. who has been handling the case since the arrest.

The purpose of my email is to let you know that, after church today, I will walk up to the courthouse and have a little prayer time around 1pm before I go and meet with the new D.A. to discuss tomorrow's events. I'll bring my candle and say a prayer for Clara, whose birthday was yesterday. Please feel free to join me in prayer at 1:00 p.m. tomorrow, either at the courthouse or in your home, to celebrate the light that continues to shine within my daughter.

I trudged up to the D.A.'s office after dropping off Jason at my delightful neighbor's house. While there, I shared the happy news that I had just accepted a job as Executive Secretary to the Commissioner of Commerce. This position was a major blessing and made me feel some strength and bravado. It gave me courage to believe that my children and I would survive. At the time, one of my biggest concerns was how to make the family work financially. I was so elated to feel that I could carry my family.

The new D.A. turned out to be a woman younger than me—something I had started to notice was true frequently, as I stepped out into the workforce after raising children for 15 years. While I was creating a family, others were tending to their careers. I now found myself fighting off regrets, as I came to terms with the fact that I had neither successfully stabilized and united my family, nor built a solid career that would support my children.

That aside, the new D.A. and I had a good conversation. I assured her that I could cry on anyone's shoulder and had no interest in bringing that kind of drama to the courtroom. But, if there was anything that I could say that might highlight the need for a longer sentence and support the recommendations of Cal's parole officer in his pre-sentencing report, I would be happy to stand up and testify.

The D.A. told me she was uncertain as to whether the judge would accept Cal's pleading to a lesser crime. She pointed out that, since Alaska did not have an effective sex offender treatment program and Cal needed serious treatment, whittling the charge down to a Class C felony could send a message to our daughter that what she went through wasn't so bad—a message that the D.A. was prepared to argue could exacerbate the trauma Clara was working through. The reduced charge would invalidate the whole family and give reinforcement to the perpetrator.

In the end, Cal's battle tactics proved victorious. Because of the length of time that the case was allowed to continue, he was provided extended opportunities to intimidate Clara, having his attorneys threaten to put her on the stand. When they'd had the conversation recorded in the library, Clara had believed Cal when he said he would willingly "take his punishment." When it became clear he was going to fight her to save himself, she assumed she would be supported by the tape recording of her dad admitting his abuse. When the tape-recorded confession was not admitted into evidence, Clara suffered beyond her coping skills.

On the day of the sentencing hearing, I gave the following testimony:

My purpose for speaking to you today is so that my children will continue to be protected from the man who abused us. My three children and I are thriving even with two years of intense legal badgering brought on by this man's continuous selfish drive to fulfill himself. I think it's important for the court to understand that prior to the revelation that this man was a pedophile, we believed we were a family.

This man had the blessings of family life, and he chose to abuse his family. One of my children once said to me, "Dad gets to be mean to you because he makes all the money." Another one of my children said, as we were boarding a plane, one month after their father had been incarcerated, "I bet you wish there were five of us here, but I don't. I'm glad Dad is gone." A detective recently reported to my husband the feelings of one of our children: "He really does not like you."

My husband disregarded our daughter's well-being when he abused the trust that she had in him. He exploited the power he had over the child, and she has struggled to come to terms with that. My daughter is transitioning into a life that is now her own. She has taken charge of her education, employment, and relationships. She is growing stronger and more self-assured every day, as she confronts the tragedy and the painful memories of abusive behaviors acted out on her by her father, a person who pretended to protect and honor her and teach her how to live.

Since her father has been removed from society, she is discovering life without his abuse in our home. This hint of light has allowed the child to thrive. She has close friends whom, for the first time, she feels comfortable having in our house. They laugh with my child. They cry with her. They love my child and she loves those friendships. Her life begins now.

Additionally, the relationships between the siblings can now become real. My daughter takes the time to go see her younger brothers participate in holiday events at school, laugh with them, and enjoy their artwork. All of these relationships are now opening up for my family.

The defendant was never truly interested in us— beyond controlling our every choice and our every action. In the Defendant's Sentencing Memorandum, on page 14, he denies the claim that, since his arrest, he has economically abused the family. It reads "Especially in light of the fact that he offered additional funds so that the family could stay in the home, an offer declined by the plaintiff." This misrepresents the fact that, though it was their father's first choice, I had no desire for our children to continue to live in the house where the abuse occurred. We successfully procured a court order allowing us to vacate that property—an order I spent $5,000 to secure. The defendant has offered support only when it has furthered his interest and desires, including keeping us in that house.

It has been truly shocking how immediately after his incarceration he began to batter us through litigation. He went to jail in April of 2011, and, by November of 2011, he had filed 80 motions that we have been required to respond to. Responding to all his legal demands quickly consumed our savings, and his continual litigation has taken up time I sorely need to be taking care of my children.

This criminal proceeding has been delayed so many times that the children have celebrated two birthdays under a relentless legal cloud. The defendant claims he is "so sorry to have interrupted their childhood," but his ongoing actions demonstrate that he does not care about their childhood. He takes every opportunity to expose our personal lives for his purposes in litigation, continuing to exploit his victims. He is armed with the details of our lives together because we trusted him, loved him, and tried for years to build a life with him.

The defendant is a danger and a threat to the well-being of others. Under no circumstances should he be left alone in the company of children. He uses and exploits people, especially children. He began proving his disregard for human dignity as an adolescent when he sexually molested his sibling and carried his obsessions into his marriage and acted them out on his own children.

This man is a con artist and predator. Looking back over the two decades that I knew him, I now recognize so many occasions where I mistook his predation for fathering. On one occasion, I went to sleep with him next to me and I woke up and found him in bed with my daughter. When I asked him what he was doing in the child's little bed, he responded, "I don't' know. I just thought it was more comfortable."

On another occasion, six years later, I walked by my daughter's room and he was sleeping in the bed with her. I just thought it was him being close to his child. I mentioned the occasion to a friend as being sweet, because it was so unusual for him to display affection. The friend implored me to be careful about allowing him to get into bed with any of the children, especially if he had been drinking.

The last time I found him in bed with my daughter was two years later. I was waiting up for him after he had been out drinking with brokers and investors. He came home and went straight to her bedroom and crawled in with her. I immediately walked into the child's room and said, "No kid wants their drunken father snuggling in bed with them. You need to get out now." I remember being startled when he got up; in most situations, he disregarded me and did what he wanted to do.

In light of these examples, I strongly believe the defendant should be restricted from consuming alcoholic beverages and entering into establishments where alcohol is served.

Lastly, in regard to #19 in the pre-sentence report: "the probationer shall not at any time possess, have on their person, have in their residence, or in their vehicle any sexually explicit material, which includes but is not limited to child erotica, sexually graphic anime, adult and/or child pornography, chat logs included. The prohibited materials cannot be in, but not limited to, books, movies, video, magazine, printed matter, computer disks or files, any encryption devices or computer mechanisms or other electronic devices that can hold this type of visual of audio material."

The defendant admitted to me that he has an addiction to pornography. He explained to me that when he was angry with me, he would use pornography as a sexual outlet. After discovering that the defendant sexually abused a child, I do believe it is reasonable and important that his parole conditions in his pre-sentencing report remain, as well as the option to search his computers and cell phones—any piece of technology where he can access pornography.

When I first confronted the defendant about his past sexual abuse, and then told him our therapist would be reporting the prior abuse to the proper authorities, the defendant proceeded to discard the family computer. In recent months my attorney and detectives assigned to our case alerted me the defendant may have been disposing of incriminating child pornography evidence.

I want to thank you for hearing me and close with a plea that you consider the continued healing of my children and do not allow this man, a known abuser, into their presence, at least until they are 16 or older. Currently, in the lives of my children, their biggest accomplishment is working through the damage that he did to our family. Help us to continue on this healing path that has been forged by the bravery of my eldest child.

Inextricably Tangled

Generally when anyone holds you captive,
they will not let you go easily. If you are ever going to be
free of any kind of oppression, you have to fight back.

T.D. Jakes
Freedom Is a Bloody Business.

Thoughts of the harm my marriage caused to my daughter and sons continue to haunt me. My ex-husband proved to be stubbornly disloyal to me and our children—when we lived together as a family and after he had had his parenting privileges removed. By putting him in jail, the court system removed Cal from our immediate presence, but, seven years later, he continues to use that same system to keep our lives inextricably tangled up with his.

After serving under two years, Cal was released from prison in March of 2013—a very light sentence when weighed against the childhood my daughter and sons had lost to his abuse. According to the conditions of his release, he may not be around children under the age of 16 until his 10-year probation period has passed.

As soon as he was out of jail, he and his civil attorney parted ways, and he became his own lawyer.

His first move was to depose three of my closest friends under the guise of gathering his defense for the divorce trial.

This cost me about $3,000, because I needed to have an attorney present for the depositions. He also tried to depose me. When his motion to do so in person was defeated, he tried to video depose me, arguing he felt it "important to see my body language." The judge did not allow this, either. But each and every one of his evidentiary motions have had to be responded to—a process that consumes my scarce time and scarcer financial resources.

By the time the divorce trial finally got underway Cal, still representing himself, had proven a quick study when it came to the badgering techniques his previous attorneys had deployed. He claimed he had a long witness list and specialists that he was going to use to discredit his daughter's accounts of his abuse. He threatened to call Clara to the stand.

During this time Clara called me to tell me that she was expecting my grandson. Hearing this news, I became even more protective of Clara and the new life in her, and I didn't want her to have this stress. However, because my attorney was obligated to prepare her for her father's cross-examination, Clara was nevertheless forced to once again relive his abuse.

Clara had reached legal adulthood by the time the divorce trial occurred. Cal tried to get the court to lift the sentencing that protected me as a victim because she was no longer a child. He was unsuccessful. He also tried to get the court to no longer label her a victim in the criminal case, and again was denied.

After Cal had completed his legal goals in Alaska, he was granted permission to move back to Massachusetts, returning to Alaska in January 2014 to represent himself and prosecute me.

The week-long divorce proceeding was its own fresh hell, punctuated with moments of calamity. At one point, Cal put his ex-boss on the stand to testify to his character. The man had been his best friend for years. Now he and his family were part of my and the children's support system. Dressed in a starched light blue dress shirt and khaki pants, his former boss stepped up to the stand.

"How was I as an employee?" asked Cal.

"I hate saying this, because I hate your guts, but you were one of the smartest guys I've ever worked with in the industry," replied his former boss. "You could figure things out in your head in minutes that others couldn't even process. You could project, predict, and quantify with unbelievable accuracy and skill," he added. "But you will never work in the industry again, if I have anything to do with it."

He foolishly put my two best friends on the stand, with similar results.

For the rest of the week, it was my turn to be interrogated by my abusive husband, as he play-acted the role of his own attorney. I fielded questions on everything from finances to disposition of family property.

"Does a person concerned with her finances purchase sirloin steak and flowers the day after her husband is incarcerated?" he challenged.

"She does when she has traumatized children to whom she is trying to bring a semblance of beauty and peace," I answered.

Three times he asked, "What did you do with my tools after I went to jail?"

Three times I answered, "I sold them."

Because my name was not on the mortgage, I had no authority over the sale of our home, without getting permission from the judge, which I didn't receive until years after Cal's arrest.

Cal didn't want to sell the house. In his mind, he was going to move back into the family home with his boys. He said he would "Carve out time, when he came back from Massachusetts for the divorce hearing, to clean out the garage." He planned to charge me for his time, and dump runs and other costs, and split the remaining proceeds with me. His big plans would never come to fruition.

Back in 2012, my attorney had instructed me to clean out the house and garage.

"Are you sure?" I asked, my voice like that of a frightened child. "Are you sure I won't get in trouble for getting rid of things?"

Following my attorney's assurances, I spent 12-hour days over four weekends cleaning out the garage while 12-year-old Andrew and seven-year-old Jason played in their old backyard with our former neighbors' children. A friend took them to the pool for a few hours one afternoon, leaving me alone with my memories.

The space was weighed down with all of the stuff of our imagined existence—that life that appeared on its surface to be so much more stable than this life we had been thrust into—a life now overseen by a single working mom who up until recently had been a homemaker waiting every weekday for her children at the school bus stop.

Any good memories that the things in the garage might have attached to had been overwritten by abuse—the pedophilia that had brought disaster on our home and torn and scattered the fibers of our family. The place felt like a stage on which we had acted out a fictional life. My job now was simply to remove the props.

Still, Cal's presence was so strong there. As was the children's—the old running stroller, Clara's antique doll chair, pictures, poems, gifts and collections of kids' creations from over the years. After those four weekends, I decided it was too much for the kids to be around and too much for me to be around. A friend helped me load up two truckloads of furniture and haul it to the consignment shop. Another friend, with her teen-aged son and husband, generously cleared away any junk that was left.

When Cal was removed from the family home, the journals that I had written for Clara went missing. They had been in storage in our guest bedroom. I was acutely aware of those journals; even though they had no monetary value, Clara had watched me write them and had witnessed them move with us across the country. In all the cleaning and emptying of the house, I never found them.

I can't know for sure that Cal did something with them, but they were nowhere to be found when he was separated out from us.

Over the following months, Cal did everything he could to block the sale of the house. He hired a property manager who rented it out for $800 over our mortgage costs. I was told that after monies were built up to cover the cost of repair and replacement of the boiler and the washing machine, we would receive the funds as child support.

Instead, Cal opened an account and put his mother in charge of managing the funds. She controlled his finances with his power of attorney while he was in jail. Though the house was rented out from June 2012 through September of 2013, I received only one child support check of a few hundred dollars from the rental income. Under Cal's mother's oversight, the house account that had been opened at Wells Fargo in Alaska ended up in an unknown account in Massachusetts.

Out of my salary, I managed to pay for food, laundry, school trips, dentist appointments, utility bills, rent, inpatient therapy, etc., all while Cal filed motion after motion to postpone these divorce proceedings.

The interrogation continued.

"Didn't you know that you couldn't sell anything in the garage? It was against the court order."

At this, my attorney stood to interject, "Judge, there was no child support and none forthcoming. She needed the funds to pay for bills and buy food for her children. If anyone is going to take a bullet for this, it will be me. I told her she could sell the items in the garage."

The only issue more important to Cal than protecting his post-incarceration financial future was his desire to regain access to his boys. Even though at criminal sentencing in 2012 he had been prohibited from being in the presence of children under the age of 16, Cal found a loophole through which he was able to crawl back into the private lives of our minor children. Since the court could not legally terminate his parental rights, the judge allowed him access to the children's psychological and school records. When I pointed out to the judge on the last day of the divorce hearing that my children were the only two children in the country that Cal had access to, he replied, "For better or for worse, they are his children, too."

The GAL appointed by the court composed a document for the divorce trial stating that, after Cal completed sex offender treatment, his probation officer okayed it, the children's counselor okayed it, and I okayed it, he could begin gradual contact with the younger children. The document would be filed with the court subject to my approval.

Cal was living in Massachusetts at the time the divorce hearing convened, and when he came back he brought to the GAL a proposal to use a "Parenting Coordinator," something previously unheard of in Alaska. In the end, I was burdened with one more intermediary I'd have to convince to recommend Cal not be allowed to contact the boys.

I felt like I had been kicked in the teeth.

My attorney advised me that the GAL's conditions were as good as we were going to get. Sick to my stomach and shaking, I signed the document. I knew that we had given Cal yet another means of continuing his systematic harassment and abuse. As his former boss attested to at the hearing, my soon-to-be ex-husband possessed no shortage of intelligence and cunning.

I made the appointments for counseling for the children. Cal called and spoke briefly to the counselor. The children's counseling thus started out with the counselor asking them if they wanted to have any kind of contact with their father or his side of the family.

I made an initial appointment with the parenting coordinator. I passionately described how horrifying this outcome was to me. "So, this man who has been convicted of sexually abusing one of my children is the same person I am supposed to work with you to reunite with my other children, her siblings?" I asked.

The parenting coordinator assured me that she was not going to be swayed by the defendant and that she could understand what was happening.

In addition to calling the children's therapist, Cal stayed in contact with the parenting coordinator. He also had his sex offender treatment provider in Massachusetts call the parenting coordinator. The parenting coordinator told the sex offender treatment provider that she had told Cal repeatedly that there needed to be more time for the children to receive therapy before it would become clear if contact was of interest to them. The sex offender treatment provider in Massachusetts had been unaware of these conversations and quickly apologized to the parenting coordinator in Alaska.

Cal harassed every mental health professional that I had lined up for the children. I could not get one therapist in town to take on my children because of the ruling that allowed him access to their psychological records. Sophia, now at the end of her career, the counselor who had seen Jason very early on in his trauma, shared with me her opinion that the judge had made a huge mistake in allowing Cal access to the children's counseling records.

In time, the relationship with their therapist became intolerable. I was already dealing with a parenting coordinator brought in by Cal who now wanted me to pay part of her fee. Meanwhile, I had to scrape up $5,000 to battle my ex-husband in court for permission to move out of the family home into a two-bedroom, one-and-a-half bath rental.

Cal lived rent free with his mom in Massachusetts, where he is not required to register as a sex offender. During this time he was also courting a woman, whom he married within months of finalizing our divorce. And he changed his last name.

By the end of his original criminal trial, he had run up a legal bill exceeding $300,000, which his mother loaned him money for. He is now repaying her $1,000 a month, while paying $441.45 a month in child support for three children—the same small amount he has been paying for the past seven years. Even though it's the children's legal right and their father's legal obligation, I have been unable to convince the state to open a child support case for my children.

Since the day the police led him away, the abusive father who promised his victim daughter that he would "take his punishment" has filed over 120 motions in court, seeking to reduce the money he owes our family and restore his visitation rights. I have spent over $80,000 opposing these motions. Cal has now appealed the child custody and visitation provisions of our divorce decree to the Alaska Supreme Court. He also appealed the disproportionate property division that the judge had ruled on because he surmised that Cal could not and would not pay sufficient child support. Recently, two years after making the original property allocation, the judge ordered me to repay Cal $11,000.

This is a common experience for people who have batterer ex-partners. They end up in court all the time, and money and housing are constant issues. Over 90% of domestic violence cases involve financial abuse.

While the initial disclosure of my husband's abuse of our children had hit me like a bolt of lightning, with cataclysmic effects on me and the children, the constant hammering blows of Cal's endless legal filings over the past seven years have threatened to disfigure my heart. Thankfully, my children, my loyal friends, my faith in God's ultimate plan for my life, and my running continue to sustain me.

Running

The soft rain is masquerading as heavy mist. It bounces off large, flat devil's club leaves with a gentle pit-pat. The playful spirits that inhabit these deep woods sing of imagination, camaraderie, and solitude. I discreetly survey my running partner. Who is this new man?

Up, up we run, approaching the concave ridge. Heavy black tights hug my legs. Our conversation only scratches the surface of the emotions buried under my skin, slowly fossilizing. With no receiver outside the skin, my story—of unmet needs, hurts, the desire to be known—lies silent inside me. How many more miles will I run with this man before my skin authorizes the release of these truths?

Sweet mountain air and uncertainty fall over us like seasoning and bring out the flavor of the day—the potential for incompatible conversation and mismatched endurance levels— I always fear when running with a new friend.

My cells are reorganizing around the enthusiasm that has begun to fill my blood. This new friend has occupied so much of my thoughts and spirit lately. Why? How?

A ring of campfire stones has been placed in the soft earth. Brown glass shards from an earlier celebration glimmer among the rocks of the outcropping we now stand on. Our eyes consume the mountainous landscape through a curtain of fragrant, dripping trees that form an awning over us.

"We should come camp here some time," he suggests.

"Yeah," I reply nonchalantly, disguising the raw emotion his words have sent shooting through me. "That would be fun!"

"Have you ever felt like the mountains move farther away when you stop to look at them?" he asks, breaking his stride to take another look around. I stop beside him, quietly catch my breath, re-oxidize my leg muscles, and take in his question.

"Sometimes, when I'm out here on my mountain bike, I sense the mountains moving toward me when I inhale and away from me when I exhale." Happily, I engage in an experiment, inhaling the mountains toward me and exhaling them away.

This friendship is almost a year old, yet it feels like it's a week old. It's work, traversing this strange emotional terrain. Hiding and ignoring fear and truth. Can he love me? Or is that, too, foreclosed by past trauma—his and mine?

Running ahead, I slip on a saturated plank, splashing butt first into a huge mud puddle. He helps me up, and we are soon once again laughing and running.

We arrive at the top of the ridge. An old beaten up edifice marks the summit. "You want some beef jerky?" he offers. I decline, letting him know I've brought some peanut butter and honey sandwiches for us.

Here on top the mist is disorienting. On the heels of our ascent, a deep fog has engulfed the mountaintop. I look down at the trail that I have enjoyed on so many gorgeous sunny days and find the landscape suddenly unfamiliar. It's amazing how different it feels, but it's refreshing, too.

The right side of my head has begun to pound. I realize I'm probably a little dehydrated and out of fuel. I pull one of the sandwiches out of my daypack.

The path along the top, though wet and misty, is straightforward. We run on. I ask my friend about his dreams, what he hopes for in his life. I probe deeper.

"Do you think your soul will ever settle?"

"You mean settle with a partner?"

I shy away from the question. "I mean, settle like . . . in one place."

"Well, yeah. One place. One person. I'm beginning to be able to see it. But I'm never going to stop traveling, and I've found I like experiencing places by myself."

Years ago, I might have been put off by his comment. Today, I can't help but enjoy his spirit. For so long I've been steeped in a life of unrelenting effort. It feels good to step into his words and enjoy the freedom they offer.

We continue to climb into the mountain's shadow, scrambling up wet rocks onto a snowy path occupied by several mountain goats and their young.

"Ooh, the babies are so cute! I want to hold one!"

Corn snow, dappled with pink algae, crunches under our wet feet. I can hear him counting the number of mountain goats. Dark brown mountain goat eyes deeply set in white fur, and dark brown horns spiking out of their crowns. They stare at us. Then, all at once, the group side steps down the snowy slope.

My friend gently taps my arm. I turn and see he is silently pointing off to my left. Another white animal—no horns, a very thick, long bushy tail at the end of sleek, long-legged body.

"A wolf?" I whisper.

"That's a wolf."

"Yeah, that's a wolf."

"A—WOOOOOOOO"

I loudly whisper: "Don't call it!"

The wolf quickly takes his attention off the herd of mountain goats and focuses on us. He starts to move quickly toward us, then blends into the snow on the back side of the mountain and out of sight.

"Do you have a gun?"

"Nooo-ah!"

"Did you bring bear spray?"

"Nope."

"I'm scared. Seriously."

He steps in front of me and reaches behind for my hand, mentioning something about the wolf eating him first. I silently think about which one of us the wolf would be more interested in consuming. In my mind, it isn't him.

If we were starting to lose the trail before we walked into this National Geographic scene, now we face a real challenge. Deciding the only thing to do is follow the wolf, we find the paw prints and walk slowly down the side of the snow-covered slope, gradually parting ways with our guide.

The snow turns into grey rock again as we traverse to lower terrain, finding our way with the help of a cairn left here and there. Images of being torn to pieces by the wolf begin to dissipate.

"Can we stop and have a snack?"

"Yeah. Here?"

"No let's sit over there near the waterfall."

"How about those peanut butter and honey sandwiches?"

"Oh yeah. Here's yours." I suppress a worry that he won't like the sandwich I made.

"I eat honey and peanut butter sandwiches all the time when I ski."

I fill up my water in the rushing stream and share it with him.

"Can I sit next to you? I'm so cold, I need the body heat."

"Sure."

Soaked through with rain and trembling from the cold, I reach for his arm.

Rehab

When we deny the story, it defines us.
When we own the story,
we can write a brave new ending.

Brené Brown

In the winter of December 2012, several months after we had moved into the rental home, I got hired on with the state of Alaska. After a year in the job, I felt competent, but I still never knew what problem or challenge was going to present itself next with my very traumatized children or my very traumatized self, or what Cal was going to hit us with legally. Cal would pursue legal actions which landed me in court so frequently that the security officer at the courthouse thought I was an attorney.

This much court activity did not allow me to move on. Walking into that courtroom didn't get easier. Coming back to work after a hearing didn't get easier. Colleagues didn't grow more sympathetic as this never-ending process caused me to be distracted at work. I was always on edge, prepared for perpetual attack.

Cal has shown a pattern of trying to get under my skin on holidays and birthdays—occasions that would otherwise be celebratory. In time, I realized that there would be some form of a legal hit on any significant occasion and countered by living my life and celebrating these days. In order to be a part of community, I had to learn how to compartmentalize. I had to actively teach myself that people were buying houses, having babies, getting married or divorced. People were worried about where they were going to go on vacation and excited about where their kids were going to college.

To me, those concerns were a luxury. I didn't speak that language; I barely recognized that language. To me, life was court, counselors, and legal documents. My goals were immediate, like get Jason and Andrew into these summer camps or apply for this scholarship for ski team, robotics camp, sailing camp. And for Clara, my heart's intent was to respond to her and to be there for her.

As a colleague once stated, healing is never a straight line. I always maintained my fundamental knowledge of Clara. She is here to bring light. Knowing this about Clara kept me steady and loving when her path didn't look bright. I knew her and I spoke to Clara, not the symptoms. As her mother, I know her power. I honored the light within her which shines so bright that her symptoms never could hide who she was from me, and I strived to meet her where she was at, so that her path would become clear for takeoff.

Cal's legal counsel pushed the criminal sentencing to fall on Clara's birthday in December of 2012. I held a candlelight vigil for Clara outside the courthouse the Sunday before the criminal sentencing was to occur. I asked friends to either join me in person or in their hearts as I stood in the pavilion holding a candle to honor the light within my daughter and to celebrate her on her birthday. Snow was lightly falling, as it had been the day that I brought her home from the hospital in 1994. There is nothing that can stop her light from shining.

When Cal first went to jail in 2011, he used his civil attorney to harass me, asking for receipts, check registers, bank statements, credit card information—all of which had been under Cal's control. His criminal attorney was busy delaying proceedings. He also hired two private investigators to follow me and my daughter around and question our friends and acquaintances. On the eve of New Year's Eve 2012 a man showed up at my door with subpoenas for me and my daughter. This type of harassment has gone on regularly since he was arrested in 2011.

Every ounce of life in me was devoted to persevering. I had no road map.

Over all these years, I have made myself get up every morning, get dressed, get Jason and Andrew off to school, and go to work. When the children were 5 and 9, childcare workers were demanding pay, rightfully so, and I was trying to work with agencies to help me pay those bills and several others related to my children's ongoing needs for specialized care.

The one person in our household who had a sort of omniscient perspective on Cal's ongoing disruptive behaviors was a child—by then a young teenager—my daughter Clara. I was working diligently with Clara's school and her counselors to try to help her finish high school. In, 2011, her junior year of high school, she was struggling under the immense public scrutiny of her father's crimes. She was also struggling personally with the loss of a key figure in her life. The boundaries that Cal had crossed created a loss of self for Clara. When Cal was permanently removed from the home, his complex system had no one directing it. The change took time to work with and the change was drastic. Even though he was toxic there was a familiarity and we all knew our roles.

Clara had begun to seek relief with substances, which soon spiraled out of control into a serious threat to her well-being. Her coping skills were maxed out. Counselors, coaches, her friends, my friends, we were all scared. She had put her hands through her bedroom window. I brought her to the E.R. and it was recommended that she go to a facility in another city. People in-the-know about this place would cringe when they heard where I sent her for treatment. It is reputed to be more like a lockdown facility for juvenile delinquent girls than a facility for recovery.

We could feel the hostility the moment we walked in. Clara ran away, out into the freezing cold, snow-covered grounds, with bright sun blaring overhead. Later, she would tell me how she felt I'd tricked her into going and then abandoned her there. At the time, I thought I had the information that I needed to make a decision that would keep her safe. I was wrong.

At about day five, her counselor called me and said, "If you don't go and get Clara, she will be worse off than when you put her in there."

I went back. I was feeling the absence of family rather acutely and concerned that friends were worn out by the ceaseless demands of my situation, but I found a household my boys could stay with while I went north to pick up Clara.

When I got to her, she was lifeless. No rage. No nothing in her eyes. She couldn't even speak. She looked different. I could not recognize the person I was there to pick up.

I brought her to the mall. We took taxis on Medicaid vouchers, pleading with reticent drivers who knew payment would be a long time coming.

At the mall, Clara could not order a drink. When the words wouldn't come out of her mouth, I ordered for her. I took her to the hair salon and asked them to wash and dry her hair. I brought her to the perfume and make-up counter in the department store where we bought her some new clothes and threw out the old ones.

While all of this was going on, Cal continued to string the barbed wire around the family. His criminal attorney's dogged efforts, and ultimately the Judge's decision to suppress the Glass warrant evidence based on a technicality, made it so that Clara had to testify before a second grand jury. Her dad, who had promised to take his punishment, was now rabidly fighting every criminal charge and every one of my petitions for financial support.

Persevering with the help of her coach, Clara had a successful cross-country running season the fall term of her senior year. Stoked by her running career, and being with teammates and coaches, she gained enough momentum to finish the semester. Despite some very tenuous days, she kept up as much as she could with athletics and academics. But, after winter break, the stress of it all finally caught up with her. Even with the school staff doing all they could to help this former straight A student succeed, her attendance continued to slip. Her grades had suffered too much and she was denied the educational exposure and opportunity. On Father's Day of 2013, one week after her high school graduation, Clara entered a facility that treats substance abuse due to underlying trauma.

When I found the facility in Orange County, California, I called my college roommate Elizabeth, from my freshman and sophomore year at college in Vermont. Elizabeth is from Orange County and went back after graduating from college. She vetted the facility.

Clara was fearful of entering a treatment facility after her first experience. The morning of her flight to Orange County, she stalled at every possible turn. I kept telling myself that if we got the proper care for Clara, she would have her life back. I chased down every last thing she asked me to do and I promised I'd come get her if for any reason she wanted to leave.

She took me up on all of it. She had left a white paper bag

with handles, containing books that she was reading, in a vacant parking lot downtown, and she wanted me to retrieve the books for her trip. I did as she asked.

Clara had to drop something off at her boyfriend's house. As we ran that errand, I watched the clock tick down, becoming ever more anxious she would miss her flight.

I was becoming all too familiar with this pattern of last minute stuff getting in the way, only to make it that much more of a feat when we finally accomplished what we'd planned. When we left her boyfriend's, she informed me we needed to go back by our house to pick up a package of smoked salmon that I had prepared for her. After I ran in the house and got it for her, she began yelling at me for not wrapping it in its skin before putting it in a container. At the airport, her friends were waiting to send her off.

Elizabeth picked Clara up at the airport. She checked in on Clara like a loving aunt, had her over for dinner, and took her shopping.

Three months later, in September, the boys and I picked up Clara—a few weeks shy of her scheduled program completion date. She later confirmed my belief that she'd wanted to make sure that I meant it when I said she didn't have to stay if she didn't want to. I anticipated this trust check, and I was entirely grateful that she made it through up until the last few days of the program. It was there that she downloaded the information that would allow her recovery to succeed.

Andrew and Jason still look back on the trip as our California vacation. We only spent the weekend, but we made the most of it, playing on the beach both days. It really was fun, and so nice to visit with Elizabeth and her family. We even caught a glimpse of a movie star on the beach. And as we walked through the upscale beach neighborhood with its white cement sidewalks and expensive homes, Foster the

People's song, "Pumped up Kicks" was blaring out of someone's carefree home. Me and the boys were just soaking it all in, this foreign existence.

At Christmas time, I organized a trip to Massachusetts so all of us could see family and get another little shot of normal life. My divorce hearing, originally scheduled for December 2013, had been moved to January 2014. Instead of relaxing with my extended family over the holiday, I would spend my time in Massachusetts preparing for the weeks-long trial.

Incidentally, my boss also told me that she didn't think it was a wise idea for me to be planning a trip because my work performance was suffering and my employment was in jeopardy. In the face of that challenging information, I booked a flight to Boston.

In the last days leading up to the Christmas trip Clara told me she wouldn't be joining us. We were on our way back on the day after Christmas when she reached me by phone. I was standing in the Seattle Tacoma airport with Andrew and Jason when I answered her call.

"Hello Clara, how are you?"

"Sooo, I'm pregnant."

I made myself put this new development on the shelf for the time being, while I continued to try to stabilize our home situation and prepare for the upcoming divorce proceedings. By the grace of god, I was offered an interview in the Governor's Office for the role of receptionist. I started my new job on January 2, 2014. The busy legislative session was two weeks away and my divorce proceedings were the second week of January. The job was perfect for me. The busy phones and important meetings called on my newly-honed skills for dealing with complete chaos. I excelled at this role and found a family in the Governor's Office.

Within a year and a half at this job, in the summer of 2015, I was promoted. I worked through the end of one administration into the next. My direct supervisor was a true leader. He drew out my strengths and I implemented them in my work. I was now head receptionist and a Constituent Services Coordinator. I had the best of both worlds where I could lead with my work as a receptionist and I could take care of people individually as Constituent Services Coordinator, and I could write.

With each small step of career and professional success I was dragged back down by frivolous motions filed by Cal. Through participation and training in domestic violence awareness, I discovered that education of judges on the tactics employed by batterers is an important factor in protecting families like mine.

Running

For the past several years, I've been running the Klondike Road Relay, a 100-mile relay that starts in Alaska and ends in Canada. It's early September, and I've been training all summer with a few of the guys and gals from the team, along with others from the local running community. On the day of the race, our team captain, Mike, pulls up at my house with a carload of men and Jeanette. He assesses my huge gear bag then hoists it into the back of the Subaru wagon.

We pull up to the ferry terminal and unload our gear onto the luggage cart. I step up behind Mike in line and get my ticket. I run into two old friends, Ginny and her husband Dave. I discover that I am hungry, so I sit down in the terminal with them and share some food. I flash on a conversation I had with Ginny earlier in the year on a run we did with a group out at Point Bailey State Park. When she'd asked about Clara, I'd replied I didn't want to talk about what had happened—that I wanted to let it go and work on creating new memories. She didn't run away and honored my wishes. And now here we are, eating hummus, crackers, and chocolate, totally at ease.

We get to our destination and have dinner in this shabby kitchen in the corner of a motel, like we've done every year. Memories have remodeled the place to feel like a haven, a place shared with good people and warm friendships. Everybody has brought food and we're all complimenting each other—because everything really is good—all of us crowded around a table on various pieces of furniture, ranging from sofas to bar stools.

Mike, the team captain, hands out our numbers and pins for attaching them to our clothes. We've got a baton containing the ashes of a past team member who recently passed away.

Finally, we're called up to the line. The relay has 10 legs, but there are only nine of us this year, so Tom is running two of them. Gerry is our first runner. She beats her projected time, placing second overall on her leg. After we follow her out of town and up into the mountains, we divide the team up into earlier and later groups.

The team divides up because the earlier runners and the later runners have a lot of hours in between. Glen, Dave, and I head out to Whitehorse, the northern terminus of the race.

I'm running the last leg. Carl will pass the baton to me. Up until now, I've been telling everyone to "relax and have fun; enjoy your race." Now my nerves rise above my playful wisdom because it's my turn to run. My focus becomes the tightness in my left leg. And then I start to worry about my lungs that have been hurting since I moved into a new housing situation that is under construction. Lastly, because I've been in the middle of moving the last month of training was spotty.

Dave teases me and says, "Relax and have fun; enjoy your race."

In the zone waiting for the baton, this will be my first time running leg 10, completing the relay for my team. My teammates, having finished their legs, are all around me. I have on a purple shirt over a new bright yellow tank top that I've pinned my number on. I see Carl running toward me. I take the lanyard from him and put it around my neck and tuck the key into my bra. Heading out, I feel my shoulders and my upright frame. I feel the power in my legs. I feel the fatigue in my chest; my lungs refusing to expand to pull in the oxygen. The air is dry.

The road is dusty. The sun is bright. A young, long-legged male bounces past me. He can't be much older than my 15-year-old son, Andrew.

My support team is now Mike, Tom, Jeanette, Ron, Derek, Dave, and Carl. Gerry has had to leave for a coaching obligation. My grocery run before the trip was so focused on the boys that it did not include Goo or Power Bars. I choke up the courage to let people know that I don't have what I need to get me through. Instantly, I have enough supplies to fill a Christmas stocking, at my fingertips.

Five miles in, Jeanette leans out the window of a waiting vehicle and says, "If you need to, slow down." Until that moment, I thought I was in the normal range of feeling awful.

Mike is the first one to supply me with water.

I'm five miles in and Ron stands out for me now, ready to hand me water or supplies.

"Stay strong Josephine!", he cheers me on.

The pavement under my feet looks clear and clean. As I begin to move into the Canyon Ron asks me: "Do you need anything Josephine?"

"No," I tell him. "But the left side of my body is trying to shut down."

"That's ok," he assures me. "It's all heart and guts when you head into the canyon."

I maneuver out of my purple shirt and toss it to the ground. Jogging along beside me, Ron picks it up and falls away. I'm on my own now.

I have heart and guts, I tell myself, as I descend into the canyon, legs moving without any thought or effort. Yellow leaves contrast against the blue sky. The air is cooler here and picks up more humidity nearer to the river. My pink sneakers pat along the paved road. I tell the tense muscles in my left calf to soften. Soften. It's ok. Happy. Happy. Power. Happy. Happy.

Soften. Happy. Happy. Over and over, I repeat these words to myself in the canyon. My focus comes off of my left leg, hip, and shoulder and is now on my heart and guts. The mountains are making the most of this day, their size and beauty majestically silhouetted against the vibrant, clear blue sky.

A straightaway. I know my team waits at the end of it. My legs are moving fast on their own, driven by the energy surging out of my heart. I fly by another runner just as I spot Mike, Jeanette, and Ron. My concentration breaks slightly as I ask Ron, "How far left?"

He responds, "I don't know. Do you need anything? I guess you just want to be done."

I smile in my heart and on my face! Guts. Guts get activated now. Soften. Soften. Happy. Happy. Happy. A light-stepping female runner flies by me. I see my team under the bridge. A voice rings out over a loudspeaker: "Here comes Josephine May, looking like she could run another 10k!" And there they all are. My team.

"Josephine, that was unbelievable!" cries Jeanette. Hugs and high-fives follow. This is IT, I think. The best thing. Tom's positive energy is palpable as he says: "That was really impressive how you picked up speed in the canyon, Josephine." Ron's smile is bigger than mine. Mike's joy and fatigue are all mixed in one sweet man. Derek's kindness and peace. Carl's enthusiasm for the sport and our team. I can still feel Gerry's warm hug as she left to start her leg, connecting her to me now, at the finish. And our former leader whose ashes I carry—he is the reason this team came together. A race director comes up to me and says "The man you're carrying was a good friend of mine. I miss him."

I smile and thank him for reaching out to me. "I really appreciate it," I say. "He was a special guy."

We pile into two cars and head for Takhini Hot Springs. Step into the water and it's hot! Sink lower and lower until we are fully submerged. Floating on my back, my eyes fill with the colors of the blue sky, yellow leaves, and green pine trees. The warmth of the salt spring surrounds my body and the cool air refreshes my face as I replay the ecstasy of the canyon. Light conversation passes back and forth among my teammates and other runners enjoying the gift of this experience.

After dinner at the hotel, Mike hands out our dance tickets. In flip-flops and flannel, I walk out of the restaurant and hang out with the team until we head in the direction of the school gymnasium where the dance and awards ceremony take place. A man passing by hands me a flower. I melt, exclaiming, "Oh, that is so nice!" Mike tells me he's seen a whole bush nearby with those flowers on it.

"Don't ruin my big moment," I joke. "A guy just gave me a flower!" We all laugh and continue on to the gym. I fumble with my backpack and transition out of my sandals into my dancing heels. As I'm walking into the hall, my team is lining up by the stage to receive an award for winning the masters division. I run over and line up with them. Again, I can't help grinning from ear to ear.

The music begins to play, and the dance floor comes to life with runners of all ages. I take the opportunity to tell Ron, "When you told me that the canyon was 'all heart and guts,' I said to myself, 'Well, my body isn't feeling great, but I have heart—and plenty of guts!'"

He enthusiastically responds, "F*ck yeah!"

Leaving Alaska

Even if my neighbor doesn't understand
my religion or understand my politics,
he can understand my story.
If he can understand my story,
then he's never too far from me.

Paulo Coelho
The Alchemist

In September 2017 I walked away from the job I loved, my community, and my familiar surroundings. I walked away from it all. Sold off my car, all of our belongings, and I got on a plane with four duffle bags and flew across the country.

Over the years since his arrest in 2011, I have researched and taken trainings to learn more about men who batter. I learned that abusers use chaos to prevent progress and clear thinking. They are aware that this is what they are doing, and they use the chaos to cause erratic emotions that make their victims look like basket cases while they themselves remain calm, cool, and collected. This tactic played itself out in the court system, and I quickly learned that showing emotion worked against me and the protection of my children. With all the professionals that swarmed my personal life, I always had to show composure, or I lost credibility. And that is what survivors face in the court system. Research is just starting to teach the courts that trauma victims have responses that are very challenging, and these responses are not supported because they are not understood. Education of judges and legal personnel regarding the impact of trauma on the brain is just starting to be mandated in some states.

Naively trusting the legal system to provide justice for my daughter, and subsequently my young family, was my only recourse. After constant litigation in Alaska, I decided that the legal system as it was being applied to my family was the definition of insanity.

In the seven years since our traditional family dissolved in 2011, Cal initiated more than 120 motions in both the criminal and civil cases, forcing me to respond to his legal action through legal counsel on a monthly basis, and frequently several times a month. He pursued visitation with our children and took several of the family court rulings to the higher court. He even at one point attempted to have his criminal conviction overturned to be able to visit with his young children. He constantly challenged the division of our assets. But perhaps the most detrimental of the legal battering was his success in disrupting Jason's therapy.

The therapist that Jason had seen when his symptoms had initially presented was going into retirement. She was kind and supportive, but she could not see Jason long-term and he needed care. She had observed Cal's flat affect and emotionless responses to Jason's sufferings. She said that when abuse is imparted by a key figure in a child's life it is extremely confusing and completely affects the child's ability to trust and their sense of security. She felt badly for the way the court case was handled and agreed to testify in court about her findings with Jason.

However unwittingly this decision may have been made, the Judge overseeing both Cal's criminal case and our divorce case required me to implement mental health care for Jason while granting Cal's request for access to the children's school and psychological records. In terms of receiving therapeutic services for Jason, this decision was a death sentence. Cal used this ruling to harass every therapist that I brought Jason to for services until no therapist in Alaska would see Jason. They refused to see Jason because "their schedules were too full" or they had "too many patients that were suicidal."

The judge's decision and Cal's interference prevented the appropriate therapy for Jason. Ironically, Cal then attempted to use the inability to find any therapy against me. In the late spring and summer of 2017 while we were still living in Alaska, Cal pushed hard, filing motions for continuous hearings to discern my efforts to procure care for Jason. Anyone, professional or layperson, could tell that to be involved with this case meant that you were going to be in court often. They didn't want to be drawn into this case.

The GAL, Micaela, was also trying to find mental health care for Jason, who was now 11 years old. She spent time with him, trying to see where he was at emotionally and just as a young boy. Because there was no progress in finding a therapist who would treat Jason, Micaela offered to meet with him herself.

I invited her to our home to have dinner with Jason and me. Conversation over spaghetti and meatballs was light and Jason excused himself to go sit on the couch. She and I finished dinner and she asked Jason if she could sit next to him.

He shrugged his shoulders and didn't look up from his screen.

"If you want to," he quietly said.

"Is that ok with you?"

"Yeah. I mean. I don't really care," said Jason.

"Do you know why I'm here?"

"To talk about my Dad?"

"Well, not just to talk about your Dad. I'm here for you. I know your family has been through a lot and I want to make sure that you are ok."

"Why don't you charge him with neglect?"

"Do you feel neglected by your Dad, Jason?"

"Do you know the definition of neglect?" asked Jason. "You should charge him with it."

Jason proceeded to read the definition of neglect off the tablet he had on his lap:

> neglect: (verb)
>
> 1. Fail to care for properly. To give little attention or respect to.
>
> 2. To leave undone or unattended to especially through carelessness.

"Yeah. Charge him with neglect," said Jason, in his prepubescent, high-pitched voice, with his small frame tucked deeply in the brown sofa, hiding the tears that were rolling down the soft skin of his angular, beautiful face.

Micaela repeated her question, "Do you feel like your Dad neglected you Jason?"

"Yes I do. Put him in jail."

At the next hearing, Micaela was able to tell the judge that Jason was very fragile and she believed that he needs much more time to heal before there is even the consideration of visitation by his father.

The culminating point, at which I did not know if another state would provide better legal protection for me and my family, was in September of 2017. The judge chastised me for not getting counseling in a town where not even the GAL could find a counselor who would see my sons, and mandated that I either write a check for $11,000 to my ex-husband or reduce the amount of retirement assets that I was to receive by that same amount. I decided that justice was not happening. We were held captive by Cal's tactical use of the legal system.

After living in Alaska for 15 years, I felt like I had no choice but to leave, I did not have the clarity to stop and think about how much Alaska was now a part of me. And, I could not have evaluated how much it meant to me to leave job security. I worked really hard to get where I was in my position. I built security for my children and myself, from the ground up. It was only in hindsight that I could evaluate what Cal's continued legal battering had cost me, as I moved away in pursuit of freedom from his actions. When I walked out of Alaska I did not have a life set up for myself in Massachusetts. I had gracious and generous family that I hadn't spent more than a few weeks with at a time, for two decades. It was a major adjustment for all of us.

Starting over, again, I found a small apartment in the town I grew up in, north of Boston. I bought a ten-year-old car, beds for me and the boys, a living room set, and other furniture was given to us by family and friends. One of my best friends from high school helped me secure a substitute teaching role at the grammar school he worked at, and eventually with the help of family I was able to secure a job that at least covered the basic cost of living for me and the boys.

Still, I was in court telephonically once a month through December and hearings were held monthly through February 2018. I came home from a job interview in December, ran to

Jason's sixth grade Christmas Pageant at his middle school and ran home to meet with my attorney as the call was underway for the December hearing. The judge got on the line and said "I'm losing track of why we are here today."

Clara

*A woman clothed in the sun, with the moon under
her feet and a crown of twelve stars on her head.*

Revelations 12:1

After reading this magnificent imagery in the book of
Revelations, I texted Clara.

"Clara, will you sketch the words in Revelations 12:1, take a
photo, and send it to me? Quick sketch—nothing fancy."

"I'm sure Chitters is coming my way," I continue, referring
to a time when Clara was 12 years old and we were renting a
beach house on the north shore of Massachusetts for our
summer vacation. There was a beautiful twilight scene of an
old pastel purple beach house with seagulls on the porch roof,
tall wispy beach grass blowing in the wind, and a gorgeous
sandy beach in front of the rough ocean. Upon my request of
Clara to please sketch that scene for me, she proceeded to
paint a finely detailed picture of a Christmas chipmunk named
"Chitters."

Although Chitters was not the drawing I requested, I have
him in a red cloth frame and I keep it on display year-round.
Chitters makes me smile in my heart as he reminds me of
Clara's talent, insight, and spunk. All throughout her
childhood Clara gravitated towards art, painting and sketching
elaborate scenes of fairies in the forest or characters from her

American Girl books. Throughout her pregnancies, she continued to paint watercolor self-portraits and scenes from the Alaskan wilderness.

Clara replied, "I wish I had time to do your sketch this morning. Will do it later."

Clara is now married and she is raising two busy little boys, 3 year-old George, and 1 year-old Charlie. Early on in her role as a mom, she connected with a program called Parents as Teachers. This program provided her with information about her children's development, advice on how to help her children, and activities that she could get her children involved in. She also found reassurance that she was handling their needs appropriately. Clara keeps her boys well cared for with lots of outdoor excursions, healthy food, age appropriate toys, and a constant rotation of books.

Clara has a vast interest in medicinal foods and herbs. She worked part time for a naturopathic doctor. She is constantly harvesting plants, herbs, and flowers in Alaska that she uses for her health.

The road to parenting for Clara began with living in a big blue bus as a pregnant teenager, and subsequently with an infant. George was born when Clara was 19 years old. She married her husband, Finn, shortly thereafter, and the three of them lived on the bus together for about a year before relocating to an apartment. Finn and Clara recently traded roles and she has a job working in a law office while Finn is now caretaker for their two children. They rent a two-bedroom apartment, are both finishing their college degrees, raising their children, and nurturing their marriage.

Clara and Finn are both excellent distance runners and athletes. They seldom have the opportunity to run together because of parenting responsibilities but running is something they share in common. Clara is currently enrolled in an online summer course for child development and she's almost halfway through her undergraduate degree. Life is busy for her and she keeps an upbeat spirit almost all of the time.

Clara also maintains a core group of close friends that she has had throughout high school. She's in her early 20's and has the occasion to have an evening out once in a while with Finn or with her friends. She loves her home and excels at her education.

We will never know for sure what the outcome would have been if she had had the opportunity to access a private education during high school, or if her college education was not her own financial responsibility. Clara's maturity and the way she worked through and is working through her recovery is remarkable to me. On her own, Clara has sought out the tools that she needs to raise her children and to procure her family's education, transportation, housing, and medical needs.

Clara and I are living on opposite coasts as I write this. It was never my intention to leave her and move away from Alaska. She understood that my goal was to confront the issue of Cal's battering through the court in a new way; she's been really angry watching me live in the courtroom through the years. Clara has rightfully chosen to pull back from the court proceedings because they are so damaging to recovery, constant reminders of Cal's power and control asserted over freedom and beauty.

When I read the words "A woman clothed in the sun, with the moon under her feet and a crown of twelve stars on her head," I saw Clara's artwork, pictures she had already drawn. I know these words will take a beautiful form from her imagination on to a canvas. Art is freedom.

Clara is a fantastic artist, writer, poet, yogi, athlete, daughter, mother, friend, wife, sister and a person who shares her humor, her cooking, her love of nature, and her light with those she loves.

Andrew

It's times like these you learn to live again
It's times like these you give and give again
It's times like these you learn to love again
It's times like these time and time again

Foo Fighters

"You are one of my favorite people to hang out with," I said to Andrew, on a warm day in late spring 2018. Sophomore year finals were complete. Andrew had just hugged his best friend, Silas, goodbye after they'd had a small celebration to commemorate his 17th birthday.

"You too. Vice versa. Or, you are one of my favorite people to hang out with, too," he replied.

"I love you," I said, realizing that I have to take the opportunity, when it's there, to tell him that I love him. Andrew and I are in constant conversation. We both love to chat with each other and share philosophies or running times. He is the kindest person I have ever met. In one of our conversations, Andrew says to me, "Mom, I didn't have a childhood."

I respond to him with the truth and I acknowledge his remark, "I know."

Then he hopped on a plane to spend the summer in Alaska with his sister, his friends, and his co-workers.

It was a huge leap of faith to plan his summer of 2018 in Alaska. We missed his sister and she missed us a lot when we left Alaska in September. She wasn't sure she missed him enough to take him in for the entire summer, but when he arrived, the first thing they did was go on an eight mile run in the mountains! The morning after his arrival, my phone rang and it was Clara calling me from Alaska to report that Andrew "did all of the dishes this morning!" It was fun to hear their relationship taking on the next phase as they mature.

A year ago last summer, Andrew and I sat on the back porch of my parent's home, talking about leaving Alaska and moving to Massachussetts. We prayed about it and we talked some more. Finally, after this went on for a few days, Andrew said to me, "Make a decision."

Each syllable heavy on my tongue and my facial muscles frozen, I could feel the words as they left my mouth: "We—are—moving."

The words hung in the air, alongside the concept of being in my parents' home as an adult.

The words had no celebration for me. Moving meant, as my mother said, "a complete free fall." The decision to move was born out of need to fight back. The freedom to make the decision was based around Andrew being accepted at an excellent high school in Massachusetts, and Jason getting accepted into a well structured middle school, and my parents' generosity in helping me afford their education.

In April of 2017, before we decided to leave Alaska, Andrew had been called to speak to the judge who has presided over our case for seven years. Cal had relentlessly pursued visitation with the boys, but Andrew, at the time, was 15 years old, so the judge interviewed him directly.

Andrew's in-camera interview in the Alaska Court
April 14, 2017

Judge: I don't want you to be nervous. I know this is kind of a weird situation sitting and talking to a Judge. Um. Let me start by telling you a little bit about ground rules of what we are doing here alright. First of all there is a microphone there on the table. We are recording our conversation. We are doing that, obviously for a number of reasons. Ahh. But Um, the recording will be sealed. Sealed means the public doesn't get to come listen to it. Ah, the parties don't get to come listen to it. It is sealed so that no one can listen to it. I can not promise you that it will always remain sealed and that at some point; for instance, your parents might get to listen to it. I don't want to make you promises that I can't keep.

Andrew: Right.

Judge: And, you know, I'm conducting court proceedings. I need to do them in a fair way that protects everyone's rights. And it is possible that if I'm making decisions at some point in the future, it is possible that folks including potentially both of your parents might be able to listen to it.

Andrew: Right.

Judge: So, just so that's understood. Um and um I guess I want just. I'm doing this to try to figure out where you are coming from. And so, I want to do more listening than talking, and kind of hear what you have to say. I guess the first thing I want to do is tell me if you can, your understanding of what we are doing here today.

Andrew: Um. I feel like I was giving my opinion on custody or like seeing my father or if I feel like it's like what I want or how comfortable I am with my current situation.

Judge: Good. Um. So let me just start with asking this question. Tell me what is it you want, are there things you want to tell me about that? Tell me where you're coming from.

Andrew: I feel like I'm getting to the point in my life where parents are guidance, and they are useful to me because I'm not self sufficient yet. So, I can't provide for myself currently, and, but I'm getting to the point where I'll be leaving soon enough. So, I feel like my mom's been great for me. She's given me a lot of mentors in many different things: athletics, school, music, and helped me build up to the point where I am now. And really directed me towards career opportunities. And given me morals, and she's been amazing. And I know this court thing has been difficult for her because she kind of just wants to move on with her life. But, for me it's irrelevant. I feel like my life's going to do whatever it's going to do and I don't need anything to change it.

I just finished a lifeguarding course! I passed it. It was pretty awesome because I'm not quite sixteen yet, but when I do turn sixteen, I'm looking forward to making a pretty decent amount of money. Lifeguarding pays pretty well and I was hoping to do that most of the summer. I just finished up an application for that. That's going to be awesome because it's good to have something to do during the summer.

I have held a 4.0 all through middle school, and I'm doing well at it right now 3.8, but that's just English, it's kind of a little bit of a harder subject for me. Music-wise I do a lot, I performed in Folk Fest pretty recently. I really enjoy music. My mom, like, she put me in that ever since I was very young.

Judge: You play an instrument?

Andrew: Yes I do. I play guitar and sing. I'm hoping to go into vocal lessons for it soon.

And then athletics, I've been running track and cross country, and I love that. I actually have a meet tomorrow. Ya, it's going to be a good time. But, I have a lot of things I enjoy, a lot of things I'm looking forward to going into. I feel like the matter of having anything new introduced into my life is kind of, just, unimportant to me. Because where I'm going is going to be determined by me.

Judge: So, um, are you at Thunder Mountain?

Andrew: Yes. I am.

Judge: Ok. What year are you?

Andrew: I'm in my freshman year.

Judge: So, obviously, you know you are a ways away from it but tell me what, you have ideas about what you want to do after you graduate?

Andrew: So, I don't want to limit myself to any options. But right now, I really enjoy math. I do like reasoning. I was thinking about going into maybe engineering, architecture or law in terms of school. And then in terms of a little bit more of a kind of throw out into the dark, is I thought it'd be cool to see if I could make it as a musician and with athletics because those are just two things I really love doing.

Judge: I guess, um, tell me, um, I'm guess I'm going to zero in more specifically on ah, contact with your Dad. And how you feel about, at this point whether there should be any.

Andrew: I don't feel like I want it introduced into my life at this point. I feel like there may be some point in the future where I might want to see him. But I feel like I can seek that out on my own. I don't need it to be forced upon me.

I just kind of want it to be like hey maybe I'm 24 or 25, I've gone through college and it's like 'Man it'd be kind of interesting to see what, how he's changed, and what's happened in his life at this point but, I, I know he's, done some bad things. I know he, ahh. There's always a possibility for change in people. But he really hasn't been a part of my life. And I don't feel like he's very much contributed to any piece of my life. And so, ah, it should just be something that if I feel like seeing what he's up to maybe, I would be like 'ok. Ya, I want to see him.' But, right now I feel like he, just doesn't, he isn't really a part of my life in any way and I don't feel like I want him to be at this point.

Judge: Ok. Um. I guess, I, um. Just to follow up on that a little bit. I mean can you tell me, ah, you've kind of answered this already, but anything more you can to tell me about. I guess, why you feel that way.

Andrew: Um, well. I feel like a father figure is just someone who shows you what's right, how to live your life, how to be a man in society. And just, they set a high example for you. I don't feel like he's done anything to provide the fatherly example in my life and I don't think at this point there is anything he could do for me.

Judge: Um, refresh my memory about when your...you are 15 now, you are going to be 16 in June. Ah and so, you have two years and a month or so until you are going to be 18.

Do you see a set of circumstances under which you would want that contact to occur before you are 18?

Andrew: It's very unlikely. But, the thing I'm concerned...I, I don't want to make it, like, taken in like, 'hey I'm open to it.' As like, 'ok. I want to see him.' I want it to be like, very clear that there could be a circumstance under which I was interested in seeing him but in my current state I don't want any contact with him at all. Ah, it would be helpful to me if, he, because I'm an expensive child, like everyone is. It would be useful to me if he, paid…

Judge: (interrupts) Tell me about it I've got three kids. (chuckles)

Andrew: (smiles and continues) It would be useful to me if he paid for more of what I do. Because, I don't know. I feel like most parents who really care and are like trying to create a relationship… This is like a not, divorce situation. This is like a criminal situation. So, I understand it's definitely not, it's nowhere near the circumstances of a normal divorce, but, ahh. I feel like if he was trying to be more a part of my life that he would provide for me like he was my father.

So, if he…It'd be useful to me to see that he was becoming a, or trying. If he provided for me a lot more than what he does right now because right now my mom is just, she's working, she's doing the best she can. But I, I have a lot of expenses. I have college I'm looking forward to. And… Everything costs money. But um, I have a pretty strong feeling that no matter what, I'm going to make it work for myself, because I have a lot of skills. I kept great grades. I intend to keep great grades. Scholarships shouldn't be a problem. It's gonna work.

It would open myself up to more opportunities if he could provide more for me.

Judge: I'm going to ask you a hypothetical question. But before, I don't want you to take my question as meaning more than it does. Um. So, I guess the question I want to ask is what do you think, how do you feel like it would play out if I were to force you to have contact, um, when you're not feeling like that should happen? Ah. Judges force people to do things all the time.

Andrew: Right.

Judge: And sometimes that's not, not always successful. Um, but I don't want you to take that question as meaning that I'm, you know, deciding to do that.

Andrew: Just wanting to see...

Judge: Right. So, it's entirely a hypothetical question. But just kind of play that out for me in your mind. In terms of what you think that would do.

Andrew: I think it would be destructive. Because I, I have a plan for myself. And he doesn't need to play...He's just kind of there. Like, he's out there in his own world doing some... thing. And I'm here, doing what I want to be doing. I feel like if I had to have contact with him, it would be hard on my family because they all are just...oh man...he just hasn't been great for my mother. And he's just constantly held us in court. I mean, it's pretty hard on people to be in court for this long. Especially when, we just kind of want to move on with our lives.

I don't know. It's... He is a criminal. But, um... More on point. So if I had to see him. If I was forced to see him, it would probably. I'm not sure exactly how much I would be with him, and how much I would be here. But if I had to go there it would kind of separate me socially from people because I would need to be there for a while and here for a while. And it would separate me from...It would just split my focuses.

Judge: What if it was just talking to him on the phone? I guess, just talk to me about how you would feel about that.

Andrew: I...It's hard to say because it's. I feel like as soon as a door is opened, it opens more doors. So I would have a conversation with him on the phone and then it would be like "oh he is communicating with me. I feel like he's ready to do this. And this. And this."

And it just, I feel safer behind a closed door than I would with...Even though it's just a phone call. It can very easily be escalated with, I don't want to use the word manipulation but...It's kind of like "Hey, I want to see my son. I'm going to do what can do to make it so that happens."

Manipulation is a strong word, but like, there's always like that "Hey, I'm trying to get my way" kind of thing.

Judge: I'm just about done. But maybe one other thing I wanted to ask. Sometimes, ah, there are cases where a parent has been out of a kids life for a long time. And, um, there is contact that takes place or starts up through counseling.

Andrew: mm, hmm.

Judge: You know there's that. They call it therapeutic reintegration, or there are all kinds of fancy words for that. But, that, the, that, um. Counseling sessions are set up that, lead eventually to, contact starting, you know, initially in the context of sitting with a counselor. Parent/child on the phone.

Andrew: Hmm.

Judge: Talking. Not sitting together. But, talking on the phone.

I guess tell me a little bit about. Do you think that's something that would be helpful, not helpful, constructive, destructive? I mean talk to me a little bit about...

Andrew: Ahh. Having a counselor to me seems like a waste of time. I feel like I have too much going on in my life to side track myself that much. And, it's unimportant to me, to have a relationship with him.

It's pretty straight forward.

It's like, you can never really close a door until it's completely gone. But, I, very firmly don't want to have any communication with him. And, ah, in terms of having a counselor, my first experience with a counselor, was just kind of like; made me feel uncomfortable. It was something I never looked forward to. It took me away from activities that I needed to go to.

And I feel like it's...My days right now: I run in the mornings. Go to school. Go to track practice. Go home. Practice my guitar. Maybe go hang out with friends. And then I sleep. And then wake up and do the same thing. And then I have weekends where I'm spending time; maybe I have a musical gig. Or I'm with friends, but I'm, living my own life. I don't want to have any other things thrown into it that will complicate it any more than it already is. Because I do a lot of things.

Judge: I think I'm about out of questions but is there anything else you think I need to know?

Andrew: I'm wondering… I'm trying to figure out what this case is still facilitating. Like, what's going on with it anymore? It's been going on for so long that I'm just kind of here interjecting or listening so that I sort of know what's going on but what's the purpose of my mom still being in court?

Like, I guess I'm kind of questioning you more than me, now.

Judge: Sure. Um. I guess what I would say is I think there's still money stuff that needs to get hashed out and I guess I don't want to go into that too much because I don't think it's something you ought to worry about.

And there is still a question that I have to decide about whether there should be any contact between you and, you guys and your dad. Those are the issues.

Andrew: So, I would be... I very firmly don't want to see him. I'd be pretty frustrated with the decision to have me see him. I don't know what you are going on in your mind about it, but it would be very disruptive in my view of things, and I don't feel like anything could be forced that I don't want to have happen.

I know you could make a decision but you can't force a relationship.

And, in terms of my brother, I can't speak for him. I know he very much does not want to see him.[Cal] I feel like the fact that he, the relationship between him [Cal] and my sister, when my parents were together, was very, very criminal. And ah, it's just kind of like, I don't feel like he's safe around children. And I feel like it's almost just kind of like "oh it's just a divorce case. My mom got full custody and he's out doing his thing. But now wants to see us."

It's like, no. He's a criminal who got divorced because he molested my sister.

And, now wants contact with us. But there's no recognition of the fact that the only reason he's not with us is because a decision he made. And I know my brother wants nothing to do with [Cal] him. Counseling is hard on him [Jason]. And, I'm not saying counseling couldn't be useful for him. I just know it's not useful for me. I can't fully speak for Jason. But I know that he's very uncomfortable speaking about him [Cal]. Anytime he's brought up [Jason] goes into like, almost a shock. Like, he's just like...It's almost like a reverting back to being a three year-old child. Like Jason just kind of bottles up. He doesn't know what's going on. Jason seems very much like a victim. Just as much as me, or my sister, or my mother were.

I want the case to be over. I think my mother has really struggled with having to still deal with this. She wants to move on with her life. She wants to be an author. She wants to work to put me through college. And, I don't think there should be any case here anymore. None of us want to have any relationship with him. There could be a possibility. There's always a door until he's gone. None of us want to have a relationship with him. I very much doubt Jason would want to come and talk to you. He's still very young. I think it would be very uncomfortable for him. And, on the side of money, I think he should be paying a lot more than he does.

Judge: What I can tell you is that making decisions in custody and visitation. There are a list of factors that judges are supposed to look at. One of those factors is preference of children involved. Court is supposed to consider that. Court doesn't do just what the kids say. There's lots of cases if you did that it would put kids in the middle where sometimes things are hard for them. The law also says that the court should consider children's preferences to the extent that they are mature enough to express those preferences. Obviously a two year old isn't going to give a preference about that, they can't.

You are obviously a mature 15 year old. And I appreciate having a chance to hear what you have to say. It's helpful to me.

Andrew: mm hmm.

Judge: I'm glad we had a chance to talk. I think we are done but I'm happy to hear if you want to talk anymore.

Andrew: I think my point has been made pretty clear.

Judge: I think so. Thank you. Appreciate talking to you. You've got great things ahead for you. You will be able to do whatever you want to do with your life. Thank you for coming and talking to me.

Following Andrew's interview with the judge in April of 2017, Andrew watched me go to court four times in May of 2017, as Cal had now shifted his focus from Andrew to enforcing visitation with his little brother, Jason. Interspersed in the court hearings in Alaska, we made a quick trip to Boston for Andrew's grandparents 50th wedding anniversary. Andrew played the guitar and sang "Unchained Melody" for his grandparents in a private ceremony in their church.

Andrew was hired to work in the Alaskan tourism industry for the summer of 2017 and the summer of 2018. He negotiated a raise and more responsibility at his job.

For Andrew and Jason, my hope was that the move would bring more fullness to their lives. I wanted to ensure that they were seen and heard, because they are beautiful kids who deserve to have fun and enjoy life. Andrew responded really well to the move. He says that he feels like a better person after adapting to this new and challenging academic environment.

Between August 2016 and December 2017 Andrew moved four times, including a new high school for his sophomore year.

Even though Andrew loved his school and his team and coaches in Alaska, he has not looked back. He said to me, "Mom, you could not have put me in a better school. There is no other school I would rather be in." He went on to say, "Before we moved to Massachusetts, I had an idea, a dream of what I wanted to do with my life. Now, I have a plan and I can see how I am going to make it happen."

Andrew loved many aspects of his life in Alaska as a ski racer, musician, runner and community member. Now though, he has plans to generate enough income to never experience the financial strain that he grew up with. His bucket list of reasons he wants to make a lot of money include but are not limited to:

1. "To pay for Clara to get an education."
2. "Buy a house for my mom, so she can rest."
3. "Buy a house for himself that has horses on the property for Jason to take care of and so that Jason has a place that he calls home."

Regarding his sister Clara, he said, "I'll pay for Clara to go to medical school." Regarding his brother Jason, he worries. Jason has a long road to recovery and along with me, Andrew took care of Jason, and nurtured him out of the depths. Yes, there was childcare and after school care, but there was a home life too where Andrew took responsibility for his little brother.

Recently, Andrew's grandmother connected him with a friend of hers who has a career in the finance industry. Andrew came home from meeting this finance guy and he was on fire. He was relaying the conversation and he started to tell me that the guy he met with recommend this test called the "Chartered..." I finished his sentence: "Chartered Financial Analyst."

A strange kind of response welled up in my spirit. I saw myself in Connecticut as a 20-something, living with my partner, Cal and little Clara. Cal is a Chartered Financial Analyst or CFA. For Cal the CFA was a three year process where he studied during the winter and took a test in the summer for three years in a row, and earned the CFA by the time he was

24. Although, Cal had the distinction removed when he went to jail.

Andrew is a very talented student. He has the biggest heart I have ever encountered, and he has a peaceful light in his eyes. He's an incredible runner and has a gorgeous voice to accompany his excellent guitar playing skills. Andrew has always had a gift for insight and been extremely considerate. At eleven years old, he sat on the edge of my bed where I was reading to Jason. The Boston Marathon bombings had just happened and he said to me, "When you think of other people's problems, you realize we don't really have any problems."

Jason

My joy is seeing him day by day,
grow, experience good times,
good food and good people.

Nana

Jason is currently 12 years old. He stands at 5 feet tall and weighs 90lbs, and he is a beautiful child! With the love support of my mother and father, Jason was very well attended to for his sixth grade school year, 2017-2018.

He has almost completed a full year living here in Massachusetts. Jason was born in Alaska, so the move was a huge adjustment for him. The tradeoff of leaving Alaska and acquiring therapeutic services for Jason is that now he has extended family around, but we lost all of the traditions, friends, and familiar activities that we had as a small family in our hometown where it was easy to access the ski hill, hike, commute to work and school and eat dinner together.

This has been a big year for Jason. I asked my mother to write her thoughts about him, because I wanted to see him through someone else's eyes. This is what she wrote:

"To talk about Jason at 12 years old is to see a kind, and alert boy. When he smiles, it's like sunshine filling the room. And, I believe that is his real personality. I remember him wrapping his arms around my legs in happiness at the Alaska Airport. I always called him 'Shark' as a little guy because when he smiled he had so many gorgeous teeth. He would laugh when I called him that.

"Now I call him Jase, or Jason, or Buddy. I know he can really talk when he wants to and he can talk to anyone. There is no doubt that he has stamina, courage, lots of love in his heart and he knows that he is surrounded by those who love him.

"At 12 years old, for all of us it is like being in an egg shell that has cracked and we have to get out of it into the real world. Jason is smart and step by step is doing just that, getting out of his shell into the real world.

"My joy is seeing him day by day, grow, experience good times, good food and good people."

Jason's Nana had his school uniform cleaned and ironed for him each morning. She helped me bring him to his therapist once a month and she introduced Jason to horseback riding and caring for horses. My dad took him under his wing and got him stacking wood, gardening, and was just company for him when he got home from school. If Grampy (or "Grumpy" as Jason affectionately calls him) and Jason were not doing chores together, they would sit in their respective chairs; Jason played his video games while his grandpa sat across from him and read or napped. Jason's Nana catered to him so much that Grampy nick-named him "Prince."

Jason is very quiet in the classroom. He still has the sleep disturbances that surfaced around 3.5 or 4 years old. He combats that by self-medicating on his screens. Often Jason will go to school very tired and even fall asleep in class. His teachers bring this concern to me. I tell them that I'm aware of this issue.

At the end of Jason's sixth grade year, his teacher responded to me when I asked her how his year was. She said "Good. I think. He's really quiet. But that's just who he is. Right?"

The results of the untreated trauma for Jason were very poor social skills, low self-esteem, poor sleep habits, and overall poor general health. These symptoms feed off of one another and it has been a load of work to draw out this amazing person who got buried under circumstances that were not his fault. Understanding trauma, the impact of trauma, is something that seems to be very new in our society.

Professionals that are trauma informed provide an invaluable resource to those of us who are impacted by trauma. Living with trauma takes so much courage. No one wants to be awkward or strange, but trauma doesn't always allow the option of blending or at times, joining in. Trauma steals a person's vitality.

For a child just beginning his life, Jason has displayed some incredible courage and grit. He was handed a deficit when he was an otherwise healthy and happy little boy. He fought through immense trauma to be here with us today. He withstood immeasurable social ostracizing over the last several years, and due to circumstances outside of his control, therapy and rehabilitation for him were denied.

It is stated that when the child experiences traumatic events, that child's emotional growth stops at the age that he or she experienced the trauma. Jason is catching up to his age mates with his social skills and academically he is a leader.

Jason's story was public, because with untreated, early childhood trauma, he had to resolve his anger on his own. His behaviors were furious and repetitive. His reputation was that of a child who was rude, mean, odd, and difficult, especially if he was in a setting that he was unfamiliar with. If he was in the classroom, he usually had a very high report for grades and good behavior, because the classroom was predictable. He did not feel out of control and he could be more himself.

As Jason continues to succeed and find his footing in life, Cal continues to pursue him through the court system. In June 2018, Cal filed a motion in Massachusetts to proceed with legal action against me, stating that I've failed to follow through on therapeutic services required by the Alaska court.

What happened to Jason is something that I believe Cal orchestrated and participated in. Cal has used the legal system like a cloak of invisibility, a smoke screen to hide behind, and a tool to keep the hounds off his track. A master manipulator, he turned the legal system into his game piece, always ahead and putting others on defense, to deflect even basic responsibility of providing for his children.

Children grow up. They mature and realize that what was done to them is not their shame or their dirty little secret and they no longer must fear their abuser. If empowered, they may confront that abuser.

Cal's own spoken words got him put into jail for abusing Clara. With all his calculating and scheming, he was not able to prevent the truth from coming out. The reason he has been so insistent on reunification is clear: Cal believes he can control people and outcomes.

My vision for Jason is that he will channel his brilliance and his sensitive heart first into his own healing and then he will share that healing with others. My child who was hijacked is reclaiming his life. Many survivors have said to me that Jason will always carry the scars, but he can learn to live around them. He is doing a phenomenal job at living a full life.

Cal

How does one cope with darkness? Not with one's fist.
You don't chase darkness out of the room with a broom,
you turn on a light. The more you fight darkness,
the more real it becomes to you,
and the more you exhaust yourself.

Anthony de Mello

"You should write a story about how you wish things had turned out," said a friend. Heat rose up behind my eyes as moisture gathered in my tear ducts. I replied, "It would be a short story; all I wished for was true love in my family."

When Clara was born, our friend Christian said, "What are you guys trying to do? Create a superhuman?" Individually, Cal and I appeared to have it all. Clara, even though she was born to Cal and me when we were 19 and 20, was going to be a well-cared for child. Except there were dark corners of Cal's childhood that, when they were ignored, lived on to harm another generation.

The huge elephant in the room, the question that I am perpetually asked is, "Who abused Cal?"

All that Cal ever told me about his childhood was that he didn't remember it. In the days leading up to his arrest, Cal, who is an extreme skier, was reportedly "Doing crazy shit. Like he didn't care if he lived or died."

After a day of erratic skiing, the only other thing I ever heard about his childhood experience occurred as Cal stood in our friend's kitchen and said to him, "My father's abuse really screwed me up."

Had Cal's sexually deviant behavior been treated when he was young, he may not have been accepted into a prestigious college or piqued the interest of beautiful women. However, treatment for his sexual deviance as a teenager may have prevented him from acting on his pedophilia and spared the next generation the torture of his sexual abuse.

The first GAL assigned to our case made a bewildering comment to me about Cal's mother, Joan, paying $300,000 for his criminal defense. She said, "If your son was in trouble, you would do anything you could to help him." The GAL and Joan had developed a friendship. Joan's son was a 36-year-old man who had been my partner for almost 20 years, and was the father of my three children, Joan's grandchildren.

Cal's mother failed him, failed his biological sister, his stepsister and failed her granddaughter and grandsons by not addressing his sexual deviance while she was raising him. By the time Cal was going to prison for his conviction of sexually abusing a minor, he had been afforded the best opportunities in the world for education, family, activities, and employment. Joan and the GAL needed to adjust their lens; it is the vulnerable children who needed support. When a man has children, and abuses them, it's the responsibility of adults and advocates to protect and provide for those children.

Cal managed billions of dollars, was one of the best compensated employees for the State of Alaska, and by his own estimation he was a father by day and a deceiver by night. Joan is a woman who had the tenacity and grit to lead as the vice president of a large company. Cal's father was a partner in an accounting firm in Boston and his step-father was the COO of a hospital. These are not naive people that Clara was confronting when, as a 15-year-old girl, she stood in front of the court and said, "I do not trust the woman (Cal's mother) who funded my father's defense to be accountable as his third-party custodian." Joan protects her son and is complicit to her son's offenses by stopping at nothing to crush anything or anyone that threatened to undo him.

Cal, the man who gently protected his infant daughter from mosquitos as she napped during a family picnic, adventured through Black Rock State park pretending it was *The Land Before Time* with his preschooler, rock-climbed and read stories to his brilliant pre-teen, raced down mountains on skis with his young teenager, was also a man who secretly used his own children for his sexual needs. When one of his victims grew up and had the courage to speak out against her father's criminal behavior, he hid behind his mother who protected him, again.

Cal is a shadow character. He hides his intentions, his actions, and his own wounds. He also hides his name and he continues to hide behind those who love him, while he uses them. Even so, I hurt for Cal, and for his wounds. And I hurt for that indignity and life-long scars that he caused my children.

When Cal changed his last name from Bering, he chose the surname "Freedman." In his distorted view, he sees himself as a victim who has been freed. He did not take the last name of the woman to whom he is currently married. He shields himself with the Christian church that he once mocked, and with his second marriage, dangerously hiding his past.

Josephine

When faced with a radical crisis, when the old way of being in the world, of interacting with each other and with the realm of nature doesn't work anymore, when survival is threatened by seemingly insurmountable problems, an individual life-form — or a species — will either die or become extinct or rise above the limitations of its conditions through an evolutionary leap.

Eckhart Tolle
A New Earth: Awakening to Your Life's Purpose

"I'll destroy your life."

"Dude. What the fuck is wrong with you?! You don't just fucking break into my house while I'm sleeping!"

It was the summer of 1993. Cal had broken into the house of my former high school boyfriend, Tommy. He and I were working together over the summer break from college, and Cal was intimidated by our friendship.

Tommy and I had known each other for years and we came from similar backgrounds. It was easy for us to have a friendship. Although I remained loyal to Cal, I felt coerced by him and pulled away from Tommy. At 19 years old, it never occurred to me that Cal would try to destroy *my* life.

My voice needs to be heard on behalf of my children's lives, and my own life. I wrote this book because I am angry, in shock and disbelief at the way events unfolded after Cal confessed and was convicted of molesting our daughter.

I don't want to be alone with this story, silently allowing such vast injustice to surround and suffocate my family. One cog in the wheel, this book arises out of my duty to write. Hopefully, my voice will move us towards legislation to prevent batterers from extending their abuse into the courtroom, shed light on the impact Judges have when they maintain status quo instead of educating themselves on the intricacies of abuse used by pedophiles, and enlighten therapists on the need to serve traumatized children even if they are going to have to give up time on their schedule in court.

Cal changed his last name and is not registered as a sex offender in any state. When I asked his probation officer if she was aware that he is not registered as a sex offender in Alaska or in any state, she replied that "when he moved out of Alaska he was no longer required to register as a sex offender in Alaska." When I asked her for his address she replied "we don't give out the addresses of our offenders." There is inherent danger in the fact that a convicted sex offender, still on probation, does not have to register as a sex offender, and is permitted to legally change his name.

"He will do this again. People aren't safe, he can't control himself," said my friend as she was sitting across from me.

My eyes grew wide in anger, and my body sat itself upright with force, as my voice moved out of my gut.

"Do you think I could have done anything more to protect my children?"

"No. I don't," she replied.

When Cal confessed to molesting Clara, suddenly I was looking at an enemy who I simultaneously cherished. In one man my mind saw two. One was the man I deeply loved, bore children with, built a family with, trusted with my life, finances, sexuality, spirit, soul, body, mind, and the vulnerable lives of my innocent children. Looking at the same form, I also saw a man who defiled us in every way.

Forgiving him and releasing the bitterness that grew in my spirit out of his actions is something that I strive for, so I can have my life, vitality, joy, and creativity. And so I can enjoy my children while I raise them. Forgiving Cal is challenging for me because he does not acknowledge the wrong he has done and the hurt he has caused. He clearly is not a man who has remorse.

A soulmate is the person that causes you to really confront yourself and your beliefs—someone who challenges you to grow beyond what you ever dreamed possible. Using that definition, Cal was my soulmate. He gave me the opportunity to recreate my life and my understanding of humanity by challenging everything I am made of.

Surviving a parent's worst nightmare of their child being sexually abused, studying Cal's behaviors, witnessing his criminal mind, learning how to function as he continued his oppression through the courts, addressing my fears around finances as Cal provides minimal to practically no support, confronting the stigma that I believed about single mothers because I am one, developing compassion for behaviorally challenged individuals because I understand what can cause those challenges, dispelling the myths that he had so artfully planted in my head about my lack of value as a mother, contributor, and person; confronting these things opened my mind and heart to a whole new world. My perspective on people would have been so limited if it were not for my relationship with Cal, as I confronted the wrong he brought into my life. Losing my identity is probably the greatest thing that could have happened to me, because it forced me to confront my belief systems and my blindness and spurred me to new growth.

Carving a new life for myself and my children is still a moment to moment experiment. Understanding where my power is, and isn't, to recreate my life, our lives, and our reality is vital to our success. Many resources helped me through the years presented in this book. Singularly, the most powerful resource that has helped me is love. Trust in a higher power is directly where my courage comes from. Through my faith I feel love, even with all the challenges, and I share that love with my children.

Staying physically active is key to being present for both me and my children. When I lived in Alaska, I practiced Ashtanga yoga on my lunch hour five days a week. The yoga class, the social aspect of it, my teacher, and the routine were a form of daily therapy. For me, it was the healthiest "addiction" I could find to pull myself into the present, take care of my body, and be a healthy mom.

We got outside a lot, hiking in the summer and skiing was our winter activity. In the fifth grade, Andrew's ski pass was free. In the sixth grade, Andrew applied for the a scholarship to cover the expense of his ski pass but when he wasn't selected, he participated in a reading scholarship program to get a free ski pass. Jason's season pass was reduced fee because of his age. Downhill skiing was something I had given up because I enjoyed the endurance sports, but I took it back up to be with my boys.

When my health insurance covered massage, I got massage for all of us, or I paid for it out of pocket for all of us. Massage therapy helps relieve a hyper-vigilant nervous system, abuse survivors tend to suffer with this, and massage helps the system recognize peace. Additionally, music lessons were something that I was emphatic about because the boys and Clara will have that skill forever, and I was looking for ways to affect positive neuropathways in their developing brains, so I made sure that they remained in guitar and piano lessons. The relationships that my children formed with their teachers were as significant to me in seeking their recovery, as the lessons themselves. At first I used funds from the Victims of Violent Crimes Compensation Board to continue their music lessons and ultimately my parents made it financially possible for them to continue music lessons.

I made sleep a priority. If I was tired, my mind could get swamped with thoughts, and not good ones. I go to bed early and I wake up early. I can do anything with a good night's sleep. I kept a routine with the boys early on and read to them every night.

I had a couple of phrases that I would use with my children when things got squirrelly. One of those was, "I'm taking a parenting break. You can have my attention in 15 minutes." With only me in the house and not wanting to scare them by leaving, I'd take an in-house break. They didn't like this and at times they'd mouth off because there was some *dire* injustice that needed immediate handling. But, my "parenting breaks" were my secret tool for keeping a peaceful demeanor. They allowed the boys to know that I would address their concerns but also allowed me to step back and let things settle down a little.

The other thing that I would tell them if I needed to was, "Tonight is going to be a cry night for mommy." There were times that I just needed to cry, maybe not prompted by anything in particular. Or maybe something had happened. By letting them know that I was going to have a cry night, they could know that I was aware of myself; and through that, they could have a semblance of peace even though it's unpleasant to hear your mom cry.

When my thoughts were filled with defeat, fear, or despair,

I regularly borrowed productive thoughts from other people. This was my lifeline. My children were subject to listening to great thinkers and seeing their books lying around the house. They used to walk by my computer in my room while I was listening and observe the speakers.

These authors and speakers were all people who suffered and figured out a better way. Anthony de Mello says, "The only way to get out of this is to see through it. Don't renounce it, see through it." The teachings provide for me a substratum to duck into while the storms rage. Facing circumstances that are completely out of my control, especially those affecting my children, I am forced to dig deep. While I participate in day-to-day life, I also nurture my soul and live in faith. Anger was the vehicle that pushed this story out of my soul into these pages. Grace gives me hope and drive and clears a path for us to live now.

Frequently I am asked to really show how I was feeling as I faced down the cruelty that I and my beloved children survived.

"Josephine, what were you feeling when Cal hurt your children in front of you?" Or people say, "I'd be in jail right now if I were you Josephine, because I would have killed a man for molesting my daughter."

My answer to the question is that I was feeling their hurt and their confusion. I wanted their father's love for them the way they wanted their father's love for themselves. It didn't occur to me to express violence towards their father to prevent him from expressing violence towards them. Instead what was present for me was to offer them more of my love to make up for what Cal could not give and to fiercely protect them once I discovered he was, and still is, a child molester.

My response to how I handled my disgust at Cal's depraved, sexually deviant behavior is that I wholeheartedly, and unfortunately, erroneously put my faith in the legal system, thinking it would protect my children after my ex-husband's conviction of molesting Clara. He is a deeply wounded, angry, and extremely dangerous criminal who is careless about children's lives. But I would never wish Cal harm, only authentic healing through just compunction.

My feelings, and my inner experiences after years of carrying my children to safety and promoting their recovery, are just starting to present themselves. Healing, rising above limitations, is a continual evolutionary leap.

Afterword

The following are a list of some of the inspirational authors, speakers, and guides that raised up my spirit and my thinking.

T.D. Jakes is a pastor, author, speaker, film producer, and entrepreneur. His humor, brilliance, energy, wisdom, experience, and ability to relate to innumerable issues, people, and places, is astounding. I listened to him on YouTube and found myself laughing, crying, relating, learning, amen-ing, and high-fiving, because he is a person who brings a higher understanding to the momentary issues.

Anthony de Mello was an Indian Jesuit priest and psychotherapist. He is the author of the most foundational book in my adult life, *Awareness*. This book, and the audio recordings on YouTube, were transformational in my thinking. I transcribed the entire book and re-read his writings countless times. I also listened to his audio recordings while I was running and doing laps up and down the hills of the downtown. His way of thinking helped me see that we have conditioned minds that limit our reasoning. Through his teaching I searched my own thinking and conditioning and found more freedom.

Eckhart Tolle is a German born resident of Canada. He is the author of *The Power of Now* and A *New Earth: Awakening to Your Life's Purpose*. I carried his books around with me and listened to Eckart Tolle on audio as often as I could. He shared very similar information as Anthony de Mello, but there is no religious aspect to his teachings. His voice is soft and slow and there is a timelessness that transfers through his voice.

Brendon Burchard is a leading high performance coach and author of *The Motivation Manifesto*. Brendon's voice is happy, light, encouraging and real. I listened to all his YouTube videos, used his worksheet to organize my days and goals, and listened to his audiobook for encouragement to take risks. I could not listen to his voice all the time because my emotions were so heavy and he is so lighthearted.

Joyce Meyer is a bible teacher, speaker and author of *The Battlefield of the Mind*. I listened Joyce Meyer on YouTube, and bought her books. Joyce Meyer has a commanding voice and a "Get over-yourself" message. I needed that message.

The Message: The Bible in Contemporary Language by **Eugene H. Peterson** and the *NIV Bible* both brought me closer to who I long to be: a person who knows that they are unconditionally loved and endeavors to offer that love to other people.

Byron Katie is a speaker and author who teaches a method of self inquiry known as "The Work." Byron Katie's writings and videos taught me how to question my beliefs and thoughts about myself, my situation, and other people's motivations towards me. She helped me see the ways that I hold myself back or lock myself in with my thinking. I brought her 4 questions with me for my therapist to use with me and discovered that I was doing Cognitive Behavioral Therapy or CBT, on myself.

Tara Brach is a psychologist and a proponent of Buddhist meditation. She has an extremely pleasant voice, she's also very brilliant and honest. Tara teaches how fundamentally similar we are and how to experience peace and acceptance of ourselves and others.

Brené Brown is a research professor at the University of Houston, author and motivational speaker. She has spent the last sixteen years studying courage, vulnerability, shame, and empathy. I read her book *Daring Greatly* and listened to many of her videos. Her work taught me how to have more compassion for myself and others. Shame is a huge byproduct of all the events my family endured.

Additional Resources:

Stop Walking on Eggshells, by Paul Mason— I read this book during my marriage and it helped me to begin to identify that I was being mistreated.

Why Does He Do That, Inside the Minds of Angry and Controlling Men, by Lundy Bancroft— I sought this book out while still married to try to understand and identify what I was experiencing.

AWARE women's shelter in Alaska educated me on terms like, Triangulation, Power and Control, Alienation—and provided the most precious handmade quilts for me and my children.

Acknowledgements

I'd like to thank my daughter Clara for her acceptance and support of my process. I'd like to thank my son Andrew for nudging me to write and for believing in me. I'd like to thank my son Jason for his kind and caring heart, and his gentle concern for me. Additionally, I'd like to thank our community, countless friends and family members who have offered so much of their compassion, kindness, generosity, patience, and love. You all made this difficult topic one that I could face, knowing that you care, believe in me, and long for justice.

All my love,
Josephine

Made in the USA
Middletown, DE
18 March 2019